This book belongs to:

______________________________

# Leo Daily Horoscope 2025

Author's Note: Time set to Coordinated Universal Time Zone (UT±0)



Mystic Cat
Suite 41906, 3/2237 Gold Coast HWY
Mermaid Beach, Queensland, 4218
Australia
islandauthor@hotmail.com



The information accessible from this book is for informational purposes only. No statement within is a promise of benefits. There is no guarantee of any results.

Images are under license from Shutterstock, Dreamstime, Canva, or Depositphotos.

Contents

# The 12 Zodiac Star Signs

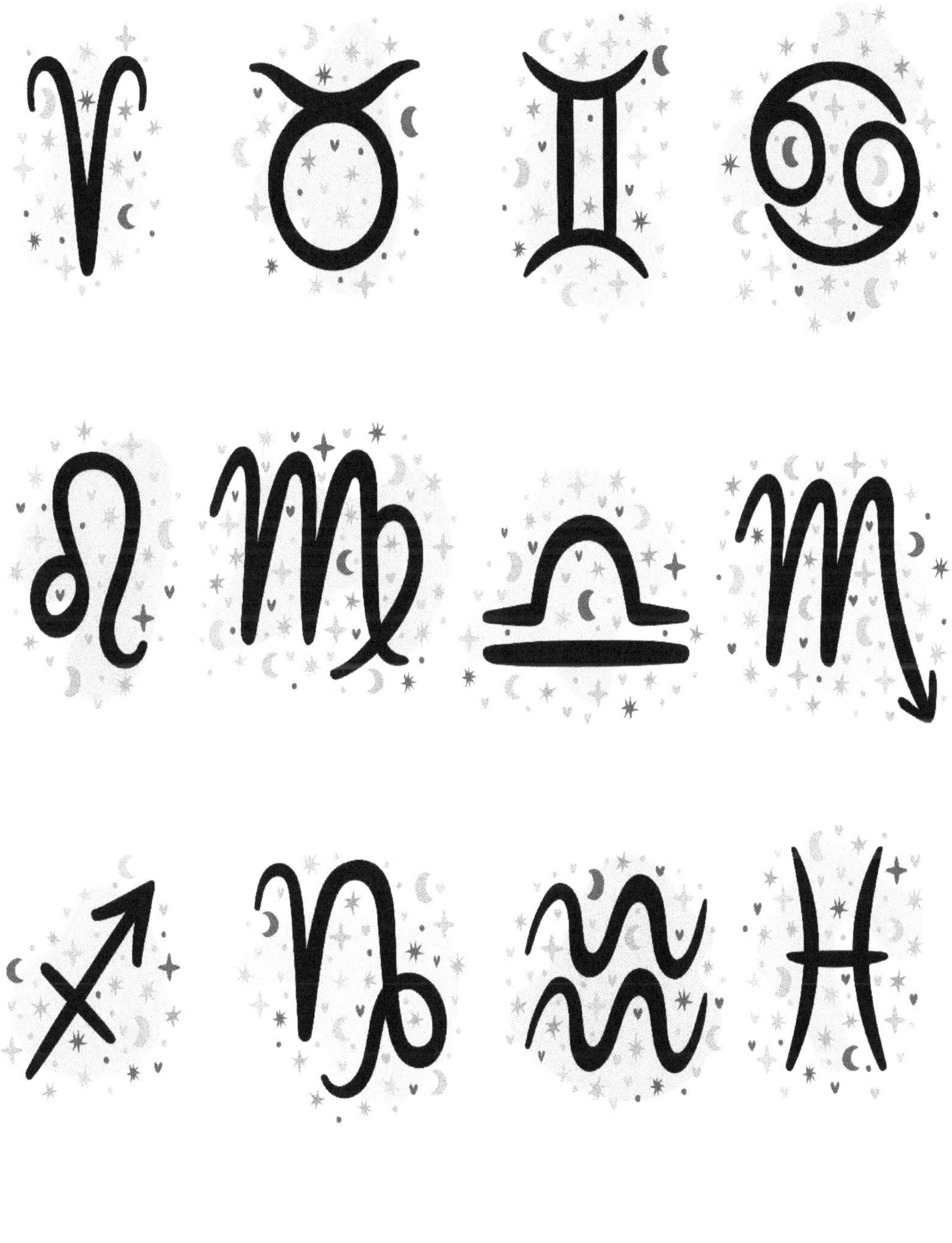

# 2025

| | | | January | | | |
|---|---|---|---|---|---|---|
| S | M | T | W | T | F | S |
| | | | 1 | 2 | 3 | 4 |
| 5 | 6 | 7 | 8 | 9 | 10 | 11 |
| 12 | 13 | 14 | 15 | 16 | 17 | 18 |
| 19 | 20 | 21 | 22 | 23 | 24 | 25 |
| 26 | 27 | 28 | 29 | 30 | 31 | |

| | | | February | | | |
|---|---|---|---|---|---|---|
| S | M | T | W | T | F | S |
| | | | | | | 1 |
| 2 | 3 | 4 | 5 | 6 | 7 | 8 |
| 9 | 10 | 11 | 12 | 13 | 14 | 15 |
| 16 | 17 | 18 | 19 | 20 | 21 | 22 |
| 23 | 24 | 25 | 26 | 27 | 28 | |

| | | | March | | | |
|---|---|---|---|---|---|---|
| S | M | T | W | T | F | S |
| | | | | | | 1 |
| 2 | 3 | 4 | 5 | 6 | 7 | 8 |
| 9 | 10 | 11 | 12 | 13 | 14 | 15 |
| 16 | 17 | 18 | 19 | 20 | 21 | 22 |
| 23 | 24 | 25 | 26 | 27 | 28 | 29 |
| 30 | 31 | | | | | |

| | | | April | | | |
|---|---|---|---|---|---|---|
| S | M | T | W | T | F | S |
| | | 1 | 2 | 3 | 4 | 5 |
| 6 | 7 | 8 | 9 | 10 | 11 | 12 |
| 13 | 14 | 15 | 16 | 17 | 18 | 19 |
| 20 | 21 | 22 | 23 | 24 | 25 | 26 |
| 27 | 28 | 29 | 30 | | | |

| | | | May | | | |
|---|---|---|---|---|---|---|
| S | M | T | W | T | F | S |
| | | | | 1 | 2 | 3 |
| 4 | 5 | 6 | 7 | 8 | 9 | 10 |
| 11 | 12 | 13 | 14 | 15 | 16 | 17 |
| 18 | 19 | 20 | 21 | 22 | 23 | 24 |
| 25 | 26 | 27 | 28 | 29 | 30 | 31 |

| | | | June | | | |
|---|---|---|---|---|---|---|
| S | M | T | W | T | F | S |
| 1 | 2 | 3 | 4 | 5 | 6 | 7 |
| 8 | 9 | 10 | 11 | 12 | 13 | 14 |
| 15 | 16 | 17 | 18 | 19 | 20 | 21 |
| 22 | 23 | 24 | 25 | 26 | 27 | 28 |
| 29 | 30 | | | | | |

| | | | July | | | |
|---|---|---|---|---|---|---|
| S | M | T | W | T | F | S |
| | | 1 | 2 | 3 | 4 | 5 |
| 6 | 7 | 8 | 9 | 10 | 11 | 12 |
| 13 | 14 | 15 | 16 | 17 | 18 | 19 |
| 20 | 21 | 22 | 23 | 24 | 25 | 26 |
| 27 | 28 | 29 | 30 | 31 | | |

| | | | August | | | |
|---|---|---|---|---|---|---|
| S | M | T | W | T | F | S |
| | | | | | 1 | 2 |
| 3 | 4 | 5 | 6 | 7 | 8 | 9 |
| 10 | 11 | 12 | 13 | 14 | 15 | 16 |
| 17 | 18 | 19 | 20 | 21 | 22 | 23 |
| 24 | 25 | 26 | 27 | 28 | 29 | 30 |
| 31 | | | | | | |

| | | | September | | | |
|---|---|---|---|---|---|---|
| S | M | T | W | T | F | S |
| | 1 | 2 | 3 | 4 | 5 | 6 |
| 7 | 8 | 9 | 10 | 11 | 12 | 13 |
| 14 | 15 | 16 | 17 | 18 | 19 | 20 |
| 21 | 22 | 23 | 24 | 25 | 26 | 27 |
| 28 | 29 | 30 | | | | |

| | | | October | | | |
|---|---|---|---|---|---|---|
| S | M | T | W | T | F | S |
| | | | 1 | 2 | 3 | 4 |
| 5 | 6 | 7 | 8 | 9 | 10 | 11 |
| 12 | 13 | 14 | 15 | 16 | 17 | 18 |
| 19 | 20 | 21 | 22 | 23 | 24 | 25 |
| 26 | 27 | 28 | 29 | 30 | 31 | |

| | | | November | | | |
|---|---|---|---|---|---|---|
| S | M | T | W | T | F | S |
| | | | | | | 1 |
| 2 | 3 | 4 | 5 | 6 | 7 | 8 |
| 9 | 10 | 11 | 12 | 13 | 14 | 15 |
| 16 | 17 | 18 | 19 | 20 | 21 | 22 |
| 23 | 24 | 25 | 26 | 27 | 28 | 29 |
| 30 | | | | | | |

| | | | December | | | |
|---|---|---|---|---|---|---|
| S | M | T | W | T | F | S |
| | 1 | 2 | 3 | 4 | 5 | 6 |
| 7 | 8 | 9 | 10 | 11 | 12 | 13 |
| 14 | 15 | 16 | 17 | 18 | 19 | 20 |
| 21 | 22 | 23 | 24 | 25 | 26 | 27 |
| 28 | 29 | 30 | 31 | | | |

# 2025

## Daily Horoscope

# LEO

As your astrologer, I wish to explain why one horoscope book may differ from another for each zodiac sign. The vast array of astrological activity constantly occurring in the sky requires me to focus on the essential aspect of the star sign I am writing for on any given day. Each zodiac sign is unique, and the various planetary factors affect them differently.

When crafting horoscopes, I pay special attention to the significant astrological aspects directly impacting a specific sign. By doing so, I can provide the most insightful and relevant guidance to individuals of that zodiac sign. While there might be multiple planetary alignments on a particular day, one aspect may hold more significance for a specific sign than others.

Considering the ruling planets and elements associated with each zodiac sign further refines my interpretations. This attention to detail ensures that the horoscope resonates with the distinct characteristics and tendencies of the star sign in question.

Ultimately, I aim to offer personalized insights and advice based on each zodiac sign's unique cosmic influences. By focusing on each star sign's most relevant astrological aspects, I can help readers better understand themselves and navigate the energies surrounding them. Embracing each zodiac sign's strengths, challenges, and opportunities allows me to create a horoscope book tailored to my readers' needs.

"We are born at a given moment, in a given place, and, like vintage years of wine, we have the qualities of the year and the season of which we are born. Astrology does not lay claim to anything more."

—Carl Jung

## JANUARY

| Sun | Mon | Tue | Wed | Thu | Fri | Sat |
|---|---|---|---|---|---|---|
| | | | 1 | 2 | 3 | 4 |
| 5 | 6  | 7 | 8 | 9 | 10 | 11 |
| 12 | 13 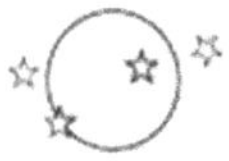 | 14 | 15 | 16 | 17 | 18 |
| 19 | 20 | 21  | 22 | 23 | 24 | 25 |
| 26 | 27 | 28 | 29  | 30 | 31 | |

## New Moon

# WOLF MOON

**30 Monday**

With the Moon ingress in Capricorn during the New Moon phase, you may experience a strong sense of determination and ambition. You may feel a greater need for structure and organization in your life. It is a favorable period for planning and strategizing, as well as for focusing on practical matters and taking steps toward your objectives. Embracing a disciplined and focused mindset can help you maximize this lunar energy and lay a solid foundation for future growth.

**31 Tuesday**

The changes that are incoming bring new information to light, enabling you to discover exciting possibilities. You open a creative journey that brings developments around your home life, which offers growth and progression. Good luck arrives with a flurry and carries a golden avenue that creates space to work on your personal goals. You lift the shutters on an enterprising time that ushers in social engagement and playful banter.

**1 Wednesday**

As the Moon enters Aquarius, you feel a sense of excitement and a desire for new beginnings. This lunar energy invites you to embrace individuality and express your unique ideas and perspectives. Use this time to connect with like-minded individuals and explore new avenues of growth and intellectual stimulation. The energy of the Moon in Aquarius encourages you to think outside the box and set intentions that reflect your authentic self and aspirations for the year ahead.

**2 Thursday**

Life is ready to sweeten in many ways, offering a time of rejuvenation that provides renewal and peace. You're taking the lessons learned and keeping them close to your heart while focusing on developing your goals. Something special arrives in the form of a message, stirring up a heartwarming time that brings a shift towards a more social environment. You're open to possibility, drawing a path that offers connection, social engagement, and thoughtful discussions.

**3 Friday**

With Venus entering Pisces, you reveal dreamy and romantic energy. This transit encourages you to tap into your compassion, fostering deeper connections with others. It's a time to embrace empathy and understanding in your relationships, allowing love to flow freely. Meanwhile, the opposition between Mars and Pluto brings the energy of power struggles and intensity. It's essential to navigate these situations with diplomacy and find balance by respecting the boundaries of others.

**4 Saturday**

During the Sun's sextile with Saturn, you can harness discipline, determination, and practicality to achieve your goals. This alignment brings a supportive and stable energy that allows you to make steady progress in your endeavors. You may find it easier to focus on long-term plans and responsibilities with confidence and authority. This transit encourages you to take a structured approach to your actions, ensuring you build a solid foundation for future success.

**5 Sunday**

The Aries Moon inspires you to take the lead and pursue goals with determination. Trust your instincts and follow your inner spark as you navigate this dynamic and action-oriented phase. Embrace the spirit of adventure and the thrill of exploring uncharted territories. Your emotional energy heightens, and you express yourself authentically and assertively. Use this passionate energy to fuel your endeavors and make decisive strides toward aspirations.

**6 Monday**

With Mars entering Cancer, you may notice a shift in energy and motivation. This influence brings a focus on emotions and the nurturing aspects of life. You may desire to create a harmonious and comfortable environment for yourself and your loved ones. Your feelings guide your actions and drive; you may be more sensitive and intuitive during this time. It's important to honor and express your feelings while also being mindful of setting healthy boundaries.

**7 Tuesday**

As the Moon enters Taurus, you may experience a sense of grounding and stability in your emotions. There is a natural inclination to seek comfort and security in your surroundings and relationships. You find solace in life's simple pleasures, indulging in sensual experiences and enjoying the beauty of the physical world. This lunar influence encourages you to prioritize self-care and nurture your well-being. It's an excellent time to create a harmonious and peaceful environment.

**8 Wednesday**

With Mercury entering Capricorn, you may adopt a more practical and disciplined approach to communication and thinking. Your thoughts become focused on long-term goals and strategies for success. You will likely be more organized, systematic, and careful in decision-making. You have a strong desire for concrete results and tangible achievements and are willing to put in the necessary effort and work to make things happen.

**9 Thursday**

A bold new beginning is emerging in your life, bringing a transition that offers forward momentum. You're ready to refine your skills and develop an exciting and unique journey that advances your life forward toward rising prospects. Moving in alignment with your passions lays the groundwork to grow your world outwardly, triggering an active phase of movement and discovery that positions you to increase the potential in your life and head toward prosperity.

**10 Friday**

With the Moon entering Gemini, your emotional energy becomes more curious, adaptable, and mentally oriented. You may find yourself seeking intellectual stimulation and variety in your emotional experiences. This transit encourages you to engage in conversations, gather information, and explore different perspectives. Your emotions may fluctuate more rapidly, reflecting the dual nature of Gemini.

**11 Saturday**

You are in the midst of transformation, and changes ahead are encouraging expansion in your social life. You're currently making great strides in developing a more friendly and lively social environment, infusing new energy into your life, and nurturing closer friendships and companions. These changes are marking a significant shift towards a happier chapter, promoting your overall well-being. Sharing meaningful experiences with your circle draws well-being and harmony.

**12 Sunday**

As the Moon moves into Cancer, you may find yourself more attuned to your emotions and deeply connected to your inner world. This transit brings a nurturing and sensitive energy, encouraging you to prioritize self-care and create a harmonious environment. You may feel a strong need for comfort and security, seeking solace in familiar settings and spending time with loved ones. Mars trine Neptune adds an element of compassion and empathy to the mix.

**13 Monday**

The combination of the Sun trine Uranus and the Full Moon invites you to step into your power, embrace your individuality, and fearlessly pursue your dreams. Trust in the process and allow this potent energy to guide you toward a future filled with freedom, authenticity, and personal growth. Emotions run high, and you may experience a sense of release and culmination. It's a time to reflect on your desires and intentions and to let go of anything that no longer serves you.

**14 Tuesday**

With the Moon entering Leo and Venus forming a square with Jupiter, you are stepping into a period of amplified self-expression and expansive emotions. The Moon in Leo ignites a spark of confidence and a desire for attention and recognition. You may feel a surge of creativity and a need to shine your light brightly in the world. However, the square aspect between Venus and Jupiter reminds you to maintain balance and moderation in your pursuits.

**15 Wednesday**

Life ahead is bringing opportunities for creativity and self-expression, with potential flowing into your world to nurture expansion. Information arrives out of the blue, feeling like it is specifically for you and granting you the chance to grow your talents in a new area, which soon becomes a strong focus. It connects you with kindred spirits who offer support and friendship, emphasizing a time of collaboration, progress, and the attraction of rising prospects into your social life.

**16 Thursday**

The Sun's opposition to Mars can create a clash between your desires and your sense of self-expression. It brings energy and assertiveness that may lead to conflicts or power struggles. Being mindful of impulsiveness and aggression during this time is essential, as the opposition aspect can amplify these tendencies. However, with the Moon's ingress into Virgo, you can channel this energy into practical and productive outlets.

**17 Friday**

With the Sun sextile Neptune, you can embrace your dreams and aspirations and explore your spiritual and metaphysical interests. It is a good time for self-reflection, meditation, and connecting with your inner wisdom. Trust your intuition and allow yourself to reveal your higher self. By embracing Neptune's gentle and compassionate energy, you can bring greater harmony and depth, fostering a sense of peace and tranquility within yourself and your relationships.

**18 Saturday**

Multiple new options are about to enter your world, and by being open and receptive, you discover leads that drive your life forward. These opportunities allow you to deepen your artistic talents and share your gifts with a broader audience. Creative expression takes center stage, connecting you with like-minded individuals who support your work, cultivating well-being and harmony. News on the horizon illuminates your path forward.

**19 Sunday**

Mercury sextile Venus amplifies charm and diplomatic skills. Your words carry a harmonious and persuasive tone, making it easier to establish connections and find common ground. As the Sun ingresses Aquarius, your individuality and desire for freedom heighten. You embrace uniqueness and draw unconventional ideas and progressive thinking. It is a time to express your authentic self and contribute to causes that align with your ideals.

**20 Monday**

A fresh wind of possibility is emerging, nurturing creativity and encouraging a fresh start for your life. The good news is bringing extra support into your social life, and amidst changing aspects, you're discovering a journey forward that captures the essence of luck. It's a time of inspiration and brainstorming sessions with kindred spirits, placing a strong emphasis on improving your life, cultivating new options, and breaking up stagnant patterns.

**21 Tuesday**

You may experience powerful and transformative energy with the Sun conjunct with Pluto. This aspect brings intensity and depth to your identity and shines a light on areas of your life that require inner growth and change. It encourages you to face your fears and delve into the depths of your psyche, uncovering hidden truths and empowering yourself through self-discovery. This transit is a time for embracing your emotional power and exploring the mysteries of life.

**22 Wednesday**

Focusing on the basics is yielding a pleasing result that nurtures stability in your life. It's bringing rising prospects that secure a more stable bottom line, giving you a solid basis to map out new options and head toward expansion, growth, and prosperity. Being open to change and possibility is triggering a path of increasing options, speaking of sunshine after rain that wipes the slate clean as it nurtures your life on many levels.

**23 Thursday**

With Mars sextile Uranus, you may feel a surge of energy and a desire for freedom and excitement. It encourages you to take bold and innovative actions, breaking free from routine and embracing change. It sparks creativity and motivates you to pursue unique ideas and goals. As Mercury opposes Mars, there may be a tendency for heated debates and conflicts in communication. Be mindful of impulsive reactions and channel your mental energy constructively.

**24 Friday**

With the Moon ingress Sagittarius, you may feel a sense of adventure and a strong desire for exploration. This aspect brings optimism and a yearning for freedom and expansion to your emotional landscape. You crave new experiences, seeking knowledge and understanding from different cultures and perspectives. Your emotions heighten, and you desire activities that expand your horizons and challenge your beliefs. It is a time of spontaneity and embracing the unknown.

**25 Saturday**

With Venus trine Mars, you experience a harmonious blending of passion, desire, and creativity. This aspect brings a sense of balance and ease to your relationships and personal pursuits. Your interactions with others are infused with warmth, charm, and magnetic energy, making connecting and expressing your desires easier. You radiate confidence and charisma, attracting positive attention and potential romantic interests.

**26 Sunday**

Venus sextile Uranus adds excitement and unpredictability to your relationships and social interactions. You may be attracted to unique and unconventional connections, seeking new experiences and expanding your horizons. This aspect encourages you to embrace change and the beauty of individuality in yourself and others. It's a time of harmonious self-expression, where you can find joy and fulfillment in exploring new and unexpected avenues of connection and creativity.

**27 Monday**

The good news arrives, helping you gain traction on your goals and head toward growth. Gathering your resources, planning, and preparation are serving you well as you enter a busy and productive time. You are marking out the stepping stones needed to advance your life and achieve tangible results. Options are emerging, shedding light on an exciting path. You're about to make a splash in an area that takes your abilities to the next level, landing in an environment ripe with blessings.

**28 Tuesday**

As the Moon ingresses Aquarius, your emotions align with the energy of independence and uniqueness. You may feel a sense of detachment and objectivity, allowing you to approach your feelings with a rational mindset. You value personal freedom and may seek social connections supporting your ideals and aspirations. This lunar placement encourages you to embrace your authenticity and connect with like-minded individuals who share your vision.

**29 Wednesday**

The New Moon amplifies transformative energy, marking a fresh beginning and a full time for setting intentions. This lunar phase invites you to embark on self-discovery and personal growth. It encourages you to shed old patterns and beliefs that no longer serve you, creating new perspectives and transformative experiences. The energy of the New Moon supports your intentions to delve deep into your psyche, uncover hidden knowledge, and initiate effective changes.

**30 Thursday**

As Uranus turns direct, a wave of electrifying energy sweeps through your life, igniting a sense of freedom and liberation. It is a time of breakthroughs and unexpected shifts that propel you on your unique path of self-discovery and individuality. You are encouraged to embrace change and embrace your authentic self, allowing your true colors to shine brightly. This planetary shift stirs the waters as the Moon ingresses Pisces, sensibly infusing your emotions.

# FEBRUARY

| Sun | Mon | Tue | Wed | Thu | Fri | Sat |
|---|---|---|---|---|---|---|
| | | | | | | 1 |
| 2 | 3 | 4 | 5 | 6 | 7 | 8 |
| 9 | 10 | 11 | 12 | 13 | 14 | 15 |
| 16 | 17 | 18 | 19 | 20 | 21 | 22 |
| 23 | 24 | 25 | 26 | 27 | 28 | |

# NEW MOON

## Snow Moon

**31 Friday**

You receive enchanting information promoting harmony and happiness, lighting a path forward for your social life, and you soon find yourself occupied with invitations and get-togethers. Good fortune arrives in a flurry of excitement, ushering in opportunities to mingle. Spending time with companions creates a relaxed environment that nourishes your spirit. You discover the numerous ways you can grow your life as the boundaries of your world expand outwardly.

**1 Saturday**

Allow inspiration as the magnetic energies of Venus and Neptune merge, and let your heart guide you toward experiences that ignite your soul's passions. Embrace life's poetic and mystical aspects, and let your creativity flow freely, bringing beauty and harmony. Embrace the magic surrounding you and find solace in the ethereal realms of your dreams. Allow the Venus-Neptune conjunction to infuse your life with romance, empathy, and unity with the world around you.

**2 Sunday**

With the Moon moving into Aries, you feel fiery energy and a renewed sense of motivation. This transit ignites your inner fire, propelling you forward with a bold and assertive spirit. You can now take action, embrace new beginnings, and assert your individuality. The Aries Moon empowers you to pursue your passions with enthusiasm and courage. It's a time to trust your instincts, tap into your inner warrior, and fearlessly go after what you desire.

# FEBRUARY

**3 Monday**

Mercury trines Jupiter. This transit is a good time for learning, teaching, and sharing your wisdom with others. Communication skills are enhanced, making it a good time for negotiations. You may be drawn to philosophical or spiritual pursuits, seeking more profound meaning and understanding. Embrace this cosmic connection between Mercury and Jupiter as it empowers you to expand your horizons, embrace new opportunities, and tap into your innate wisdom.

**4 Tuesday**

With the Moon moving into Taurus, Venus transitioning into Aries, and Jupiter turning direct, you are entering a phase of increased stability, passion, and expansion. The grounding influence of the Taurus Moon invites you to find comfort and security in your surroundings. Venus in Aries adds a touch of boldness and assertiveness to your relationships and personal desires, inspiring you to pursue your passions with confidence and enthusiasm.

**5 Wednesday**

This upcoming period, marked by a surge in your career, is encouraging you to take a leap of faith into uncharted territory, resulting in a pleasing outcome. Prospects are growing as you expand your horizons and learn in a new area, while your belief and passion for the path ahead are breathing new life into your career. Luck and inspiration are carrying you toward change and growth, advancing your career path and opening doors to new opportunities.

**6 Thursday**

With the Moon transitioning into Gemini, you enter a phase of intellectual curiosity, adaptability, and social engagement. Your mind becomes active and receptive, eager to explore new ideas and engage in stimulating conversations. You find joy in learning, gathering information, and connecting with others intellectually. You may feel more friendly and inclined to seek diverse experiences and perspectives.

**7 Friday**

Venus's sextile Pluto aspect encourages you to dive beneath the surface and explore your desires and passions. It brings forth an opportunity for personal growth and transformation through your relationships, allowing you to forge solid and authentic bonds. You may find yourself drawn to experiences and people that evoke a sense of mystery and intensity. This aspect empowers you to embrace your power and uncover hidden parts of yourself and others.

**8 Saturday**

As the Moon moves into Cancer, you may notice a deepening of emotions and a stronger connection to your intuition. Your focus turns towards home, family, and creating a sense of emotional security in your life. You may need to nurture and care for yourself and your loved ones. This transit is a time to honor your emotions and create a safe space to express your feelings freely. Your intuition guides you toward making choices that align with your emotional well-being.

**9 Sunday**

With the Sun and Mercury coming together, your mind is sharp, and your communication skills are on point. This alignment empowers you to express yourself confidently and clearly, making it an ideal time for meaningful conversations, presentations, or sharing your ideas. Meanwhile, the harmonious trine between Mars and Saturn brings productive and disciplined energy to your actions.

**10 Monday**

Moon ingress Leo. It's a favorable period for pursuing creative projects, engaging in playful activities, and seeking the spotlight. Embrace your inner lion and let your light shine brightly for all to see. Your enthusiasm and zest for life are contagious, inspiring those around you and creating a joyful atmosphere. Use this lunar energy to express yourself authentically and confidently, allowing your unique personality to take center stage.

**11 Tuesday**

Embrace the winds of change and use them as catalysts for personal growth and transformation. Stay adaptable and open-minded, as this encourages you to step outside your comfort zone and explore uncharted territory. Embrace the excitement and unpredictability of the Sun square Uranus, and allow it to awaken new possibilities. This aspect brings forth an energy of unpredictability and disruption, challenging the status quo and pushing you to explore the uncharted.

**12 Wednesday**

During a Full Moon, the Sun and Moon are in opposition, creating a heightened sense of energy and illumination. It is a time of culmination and completion, where emotions run high and intentions set during the New Moon come to fruition. The Full Moon invites you to reflect on your progress, celebrate achievements, and release anything that no longer serves your highest good. It illuminates areas that require balance and clarifies any challenges you may face.

**13 Thursday**

As the Moon moves into Virgo, it brings practical and analytical energy to your life. This transit is a time to focus on your daily routines' details, organization, and efficiency. You may be inclined to pay attention to the small tasks that contribute to your overall well-being and productivity. Use this period to declutter your physical and mental space, prioritize your responsibilities, and fine-tune your plans.

# FEBRUARY

**14 Friday**

As Mercury moves into Pisces, a dreamy and romantic energy infuses the air. This celestial alignment enhances your ability to express love and affection in imaginative and heartfelt ways. Your communication style becomes more sensitive, intuitive, and empathetic, allowing you to connect deeply with others emotionally. You may find yourself drawn to poetic expressions, creative gestures, and acts of compassion that demonstrate your affection.

**15 Saturday**

As the Moon enters Libra, a harmonious and diplomatic atmosphere envelops you. Your focus shifts towards creating balance and fairness in your relationships and surroundings. You naturally seek harmony and cooperation, striving to find common ground and understanding with others. This transit encourages you to consider different perspectives and weigh the needs and desires of yourself and those around you.

**16 Sunday**

A social aspect ahead puts fresh wind in your sails. It brings a time of lively discussions and stimulating conversations that promote creativity. A leap of faith broadens horizons and marks the beginning of a journey that attracts a pleasing outcome. Sharing with friends adds a dash of spice and excitement that brings new flavors into your social life. It underscores the energy of magic that surrounds your world as the borders of your life dissolve, bringing possibilities that inspire change.

# FEBRUARY

**17 Monday**

Fantastic news on the horizon brings a refreshing perspective. Pursuing your dreams positions you perfectly for growth, leading to higher prospects. You'll embark on an exciting journey backed by stimulating new opportunities that boost your confidence. Socializing with your extended circle of friends helps you establish strong bonds, and your willingness to share openly with others draws happiness and harmony into your world.

**18 Tuesday**

As the Moon enters Scorpio, you may notice a deepening of emotions and an intensified desire for self-discovery and transformation. This transit invites you to delve beneath the surface and explore the hidden realms of your psyche. You may find yourself drawn to introspection and reflective activities, seeking to uncover the deeper meaning behind your experiences. It's a powerful time to embrace vulnerability and the shadows within you, as they hold valuable insights.

**19 Wednesday**

The forthcoming changes are shifting your focus forward, introducing new options that facilitate growth and stability in your life. These possibilities are supporting your ongoing evolution and advancement toward new goals and rising prospects, helping you chart a course toward a fantastic future for your dreams. Nurturing your abilities brings a defining moment as it provides an open road of potential, awakening a renewed sense of purpose.

**20 Thursday**

Moon ingress Sagittarius. Mercury Square Jupiter. Use this energy to engage in open-minded discussions, share ideas, and expand your mental boundaries. Stay mindful of the potential for overindulgence or exaggeration, as the square aspect calls for a healthy dose of realism. By finding the right balance between optimism and practicality, you can make the most of this dynamic combination of energies and embark on a path of personal and intellectual growth.

**21 Friday**

You are entering an exhilarating phase, brimming with activity that breathes new life into your social sphere. The introduction of fresh energy strengthens interpersonal bonds, and a change of pace draws invitations to mingle. This transition allows you to spend quality time with friends and cherished companions. As the wheel of fortune turns in your favor, you'll witness a positive impact on your life, elevating your sense of security.

**22 Saturday**

As the Moon enters Capricorn, you head towards a more grounded and practical approach to life. Capricorn's energy emphasizes responsibility, discipline, and long-term planning. It encourages you to focus on your goals and take steps toward achieving them. It is a time to prioritize your commitments and establish a solid foundation for success. You find yourself attuned to your professional ambitions and willing to make the necessary effort to reach new heights.

**23 Sunday**

News arrives, cracking the code to a bright chapter. You claim a basket of good fortune that promises excellent results, motivating you to enhance your home life and establish sound foundations, ushering in stability and security. Your involvement initiates a transformative process, rekindling your vitality as it fuels growing creativity, allowing you to explore new possibilities. This change creates the perfect platform for expressing your artistic side.

**24 Monday**

As Mars turns direct, you can feel a surge of forward-moving energy and a renewed sense of motivation. Mars, the planet of action and drive, will push you toward your goals with increased momentum. This shift brings a sense of empowerment and a stronger focus on taking decisive action in various areas of your life. You may find that obstacles and delays start to clear, allowing you to move ahead with greater confidence and assertiveness.

**25 Tuesday**

As the Moon moves into Aquarius, you may feel a shift in your emotional landscape, bringing a sense of detachment and intellectual focus. This lunar ingress encourages you to embrace your individuality and explore unconventional ideas. Simultaneously, Mercury conjunct Saturn makes your mind disciplined and attuned to practical matters. This alignment enhances your ability to concentrate, analyze, and make well-thought-out decisions.

**26 Wednesday**

Life gathers pace as change and opportunity are on the horizon, aligning you with the growth. Seizing the moment, you can take proactive measures to put your plans into action. An important message provides a missing piece of the puzzle, leading to a meaningful conversation that fills in the gaps. Clearing away old energy creates a refreshing landscape, setting the stage for your growth plans. Newly found determination drives you toward the realization of your vision.

**27 Thursday**

As the Moon enters Pisces, gentle and dreamy energy envelops your emotions. You may be more attuned to your intuition, imagination, and compassion. This transit encourages you to dive into your feelings, allowing for introspection and a heightened empathy toward others. Meanwhile, the sextile between Mercury and Uranus sparks intellectual excitement and innovative thinking. You may experience sudden flashes of insight and creative inspiration.

# March

| Sun | Mon | Tue | Wed | Thu | Fri | Sat |
|---|---|---|---|---|---|---|
| | | | | | | 1 |
| 2 | 3 | 4 | 5 | 6  | 7 | 8 |
| 9 | 10 | 11 | 12 | 13 | 14 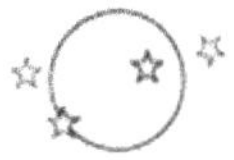 | 15 |
| 16 | 17 | 18 | 19 | 20 | 21 | 22  |
| 23 | 24 | 25 | 26 | 27 | 28 | 29  |
| 30 | 31 | | | | | |

## NEW MOON

## Worm Moon

# FEBRUARY/MARCH

**28 Friday**

During the New Moon, you reveal a fresh start and a blank canvas to manifest your intentions and set new goals. This lunar phase marks the beginning of a new lunar cycle and symbolizes a time of initiation and planting seeds for the future. It's a potent period for self-reflection and setting intentions aligned with your deepest desires. You can connect with your inner wisdom and align your actions with your authentic self.

---

**1 Saturday**

As the Moon moves into fiery Aries, you may feel a surge of energy and motivation coursing through your veins. This dynamic and assertive energy ignites a spark within you, fueling your passions and propelling you forward with enthusiasm and confidence. It's a time to embrace individuality, take bold action, and fearlessly pursue your goals. The Aries Moon encourages you to trust your instincts, be decisive, and step into leadership roles.

---

**2 Sunday**

During Venus retrograde, it's a time for you to reflect on your relationships, values, and desires. You may find yourself revisiting past experiences and reevaluating what truly matters to you in matters of the heart. With Mercury conjunct with Neptune, your intuition and imagination heighten, allowing you to tap into deeper realms of creativity and spiritual awareness. However, the Sun square Jupiter creates tension between expansion and practicality.

---

# March

### 3 Monday

Your emotions may become more steady and focused, and you may find pleasure in simple pleasures and sensual experiences. This combination of fiery Mercury in Aries and earthy Moon in Taurus offers a harmonious blend of assertiveness and stability, enabling you to communicate your needs and desires effectively while staying rooted in the present moment. Embrace this energy to take inspired action and build a solid foundation for your goals.

### 4 Tuesday

Today's focus centers on achieving stability and advancing your goals. This period presents opportunities for you to grow and expand your skills, so stay open to enriching your life. These new beginnings ignite your creative instincts, allowing you to cultivate innovative projects. By tapping into your ability to manifest personal goals, you awaken to a surge of inspiration, introducing a realm of possibilities.

### 5 Wednesday

As the Moon enters Gemini, your emotions become adaptable and curious, seeking intellectual stimulation and social interaction. You seek mental stimulation and enjoy engaging in conversations that expand knowledge and perspective. With Mercury forming a sextile aspect to Pluto, your communication takes on a more profound quality. Your words carry intensity and insight, and you have a knack for uncovering hidden truths and delving into complex topics.

### 6 Thursday

Proactivity remains your key to making tangible progress at a satisfying pace. With increasing opportunities, you're called to take action, emphasizing the improvement of your life circumstances. A host of new responsibilities lead you down pathways for advancing your unique talents. A unique opportunity stands before you, promising to expand your life into uncharted territory. As you turn the corner, prepare to embark on a winning chapter filled with rising prospects.

**7 Friday**

Moon ingress Cancer. This lunar transit encourages you to prioritize self-care and nurture your emotional well-being. You may feel a stronger desire for comfort and security, seeking solace in familiar surroundings and the company of loved ones. It's a time to honor and express your emotions, allowing yourself to be vulnerable and open-hearted. Trust your instincts and listen to the wisdom of your inner voice as you navigate the ebb and flow of your emotions during this lunar phase.

**8 Saturday**

When the Sun forms a harmonious trine with Mars, you can expect a surge of vitality, confidence, and motivation. This alignment ignites your inner fire and propels you to take bold actions and enthusiastically pursue your goals. You feel a strong sense of self-assurance and are ready to assert yourself in various areas of your life. This transit is a good time for initiating new projects, tackling challenges head-on, and claiming individuality.

**9 Sunday**

Moon ingress Leo offers a desire for recognition and validation, and finding healthy outlets to express your emotions is essential. Allow yourself to indulge in activities that ignite your passion and spark your inner spark. Your warmth and generosity are contagious; you can inspire and uplift others with positive energy. Embrace this lunar energy and let your inner fire shine brightly, illuminating your path and inviting others to join your joyful and vibrant journey.

**10 Monday**

A lovely trend is emerging, promoting expansion in your life and giving you the opportunity to work with your creativity. As you pursue rising prospects, a sense of hope and optimism infuse new projects and activities with energy. Understanding your purpose unlocks the door to an enterprising period focused on harnessing your abilities. Plentiful possibilities surround you as new options spark growth. The offering on the horizon rewards with a positive influence.

**11 Tuesday**

When Mercury aligns with Venus, your communication style becomes more refined and persuasive, allowing you to express your thoughts and feelings gracefully and eloquently. This alignment enhances your ability to connect with others more profoundly, fostering harmonious and meaningful interactions. You possess a heightened sense of diplomacy and tact, making navigating social situations more manageable and finding common ground with those around you.

**12 Wednesday**

As the Moon moves into Virgo, you may notice a heightened sense of practicality and attention to detail in your life. Your focus turns toward organization, efficiency, and getting things in order. With the Sun forming in conjunction with Saturn, a sense of discipline and responsibility permeates your actions and decisions. You are motivated to tackle tasks with precision and diligence, understanding the importance of structure and long-term planning.

**13 Thursday**

Upcoming information initiates change, ushering in a busy period that brings you in contact with your extended circle of friends. Expect your creativity to soar as momentum increases in your social life, promoting networking with like-minded individuals. Engaging in discussions and making decisions revolve around the growth of your life, allowing you to connect with friends and explore incoming social opportunities.

# MARCH

## 14 Friday

The Full Moon illuminates areas of your life that require attention and brings to light any imbalances or unresolved issues. It invites you to reflect on your personal and professional relationships and seek harmony and cooperation. The Sun's sextile with Uranus infuses this time with excitement and possibility, urging you to embrace change, explore new ideas, and step outside your comfort zone. With the Moon entering Libra, you are inclined to cultivate harmonious connections.

## 15 Saturday

When Mercury turns retrograde, it signals a period of introspection and reflection for you. You find that communication and decision-making require extra caution during this time. It's essential to double-check details, clarify misunderstandings, and be mindful of potential miscommunications. This retrograde phase invites you to slow down and review your plans, projects, and relationships. It's a time to revisit unfinished tasks, tie up loose ends, and reassess goals.

## 16 Sunday

Exciting new energy surges, initiating an expressive phase that offers renewal and rejuvenation. It opens the doors to a journey that brings social engagement and happiness. Sharing with kindred spirits sparks brainstorming sessions, providing opportunities for collaboration. This newfound motivation fuels expansion in your life and taps into a creative vibe that cracks the code to rising prospects. A refreshing change of pace offers a winning chapter into view.

### 17 Monday

When the Moon enters Scorpio, it brings intense energy to your emotional landscape. You may find yourself delving into your feelings and desires, seeking a greater understanding of your innermost self. This transit is a time of heightened intuition and emotional sensitivity, where you may uncover hidden truths and the layers of your subconscious. It is an opportunity to transform and release any emotional baggage or attachments that no longer serve you.

### 18 Tuesday

The wheel of fortune is turning, bringing forth opportunities that offer you the chance to expand your skills. You'll encounter a project that invites greater creativity and depth, yielding impressive results that enhance your abilities. A positive influence promises expansion and gain, contributing to the improvement of your life's security. This shift guides you toward outcomes that lead to pleasing results. Continuing to develop your abilities heightens your artistic expression.

### 19 Wednesday

As the Moon enters Sagittarius, it ignites a sense of adventure and expansion within you. You may strongly desire to explore new horizons, both internally and externally. This lunar influence encourages you to broaden your perspective and seek higher truths. Paired with the Sun's conjunction with Neptune, your imagination and intuition are heightened, allowing you to tap into a more profound sense of spirituality and connectedness.

### 20 Thursday

As the Sun enters Aries and the Vernal Equinox marks the beginning of spring, a surge of energy and vitality ignites within you. You feel a renewed sense of purpose and a strong urge to take action. It is a time of fresh starts, new beginnings, and stepping into your power. The fiery energy of Aries empowers you to assert yourself and confidently pursue your passions. The Vernal Equinox symbolizes a perfect balance between day and night, reminding you to find harmony.

**21 Friday**

Venus sextile Pluto is a time to delve into the hidden aspects of your relationships, uncovering secret desires and strengthening emotional connections. You can create meaningful and transformative experiences in your interactions with others. This aspect encourages you to explore the depths of your passions and desires, empowering you to make profound and lasting connections. Trust in the transformative power of love and allow it to guide a journey of self-discovery.

**22 Saturday**

When the Moon ingresses Capricorn, you may experience a shift in your emotional landscape towards a more practical and disciplined approach. Capricorn's influence brings a sense of responsibility and a focus on long-term goals. You will likely prioritize stability, achievement, and success during this time. You may feel motivated to organize your life, set clear boundaries, and work diligently towards your aspirations.

**23 Sunday**

When the Sun conjuncts Venus, you experience a harmonious alignment between your core self and the planet of love and beauty. This celestial dance brings radiant energy that enhances your magnetism and charm. You may find yourself more attuned to matters of the heart, seeking meaningful connections and deepening existing relationships. Simultaneously, with the Sun sextile Pluto, you are empowered to dive deeper into your transformation and growth.

**24 Monday**

When the Moon ingresses Aquarius, and the Sun is conjunct with Mercury, you may experience a desire for social connection. Aquarius is an air sign known for its innovative and independent nature, while the Sun conjunct Mercury amplifies communication and mental clarity. You will likely feel more open-minded and receptive to new ideas and perspectives during this time. Your thoughts and conversations may revolve around progressive concepts and intellectual pursuits.

**25 Tuesday**

When Mercury sextiles Pluto, you can delve deep into the realm of your thoughts and uncover hidden insights and profound understanding. This aspect enhances your ability to penetrate beneath the surface and access life's underlying truths and mysteries. Your mind becomes sharper and capable of unearthing hidden knowledge and motivations. You possess an innate ability to research, investigate, and analyze information, allowing you to reveal transformative insights.

**26 Wednesday**

When the Moon moves into Pisces, you may feel a shift in your emotional landscape. It is a time of heightened sensitivity and a deep connection to your intuition. You may find yourself more attuned to the emotions of others, offering a compassionate and understanding presence. It's a period for exploring your inner world and tapping into your creative and imaginative side. You may draw artistic pursuits and spiritual practices or seek solace in quiet reflection.

**27 Thursday**

Black Moon ingress Scorpio. Venus ingress Pisces. Venus conjunct Neptune. It's a time to explore the realms of fantasy, imagination, and unconditional love. Embrace the mystical allure of this cosmic dance and the currents of passion and divine inspiration. Trust intuition and let your heart guide you to experiences that awaken your soul and expand your consciousness. It is a period for surrendering to the infinite possibilities of love and exploring the mysteries of desires.

**28 Friday**

Moon ingress Aries. Embrace the pioneering spirit of Aries as you fearlessly navigate through any challenges that come your way. Allow the energy of this Moon to fuel your ambitions and inspire you to step outside of your comfort zone. It's a time for embracing your individuality, asserting your needs, and embracing the exhilarating journey ahead. Let the Moon in Aries guide you through self-discovery and personal growth.

**29 Saturday**

As the Moon aligns with the Sun, you can tap into the energy of renewal and transformation. Reflect on what you desire and plant your dreams' seeds. Take a moment to connect with your inner self and envision the life you want to create. Embrace the energy of the New Moon and trust in the power of your intentions as you embark on this new lunar cycle. Let yourself let go of what no longer serves you, and welcome the potential for growth, abundance, and positive change.

**30 Sunday**

As Mercury enters Pisces and aligns with Neptune, the realm of imagination and intuition amplifies. Your mind becomes attuned to the subtle nuances of emotions and spiritual insights. It is when your thoughts and communication take on a dreamy and poetic quality, allowing you to express yourself more imaginatively and compassionately. With Neptune's ingress into Aries, there is a sense of awakening and a desire to explore new realms of self-expression and creativity.

# April

| Sun | Mon | Tue | Wed | Thu | Fri | Sat |
|---|---|---|---|---|---|---|
| | | 1 | 2 | 3 | 4 | 5 |
| 6 | 7 | 8 | 9 | 10 | 11 | 12 |
| 13 | 14 | 15 | 16 | 17 | 18 | 19 |
| 20 | 21 | 22 | 23 | 24 | 25 | 26 |
| 27 | 28 | 29 | 30 | | | |

# NEW MOON

## PINK MOON

**31 Monday**

News of a fresh cycle empowers you to release old patterns blocking progress, offering advancement in your life. This shift reawakens your awareness of what is possible when you extend your reach and dive into an empowering chapter, increasing your career dreams. Setting goals and creating plans reaps fruitful results, allowing you to tackle high-level assignments that deepen your talents and refine your skills, unveiling a promising realm in your working life.

**1 Tuesday**

Moon ingress Gemini is a time to embrace your natural curiosity, indulge in learning, and expand your mental horizons. Embrace the versatility and quick-wittedness of Gemini, allowing it to fuel your communication skills and enhance your ability to express yourself clearly and persuasively. Use this lunar energy to stimulate discussions, absorb knowledge, and foster connections that nourish your mind and soul.

**2 Wednesday**

Methodically exploring new options helps you unearth a lead worth further investigation. You're discovering a unique pathway that offers growth and nurtures the development of your talents in a new area. Changes ahead help you promote creative solutions and increase the potential possible in your world, preparing your life for a new and exciting chapter. Life becomes smoother as you head towards a brighter future, introducing a wave of refreshing potential.

**3 Thursday**

As the Moon enters Cancer, you may notice a heightened sense of emotional sensitivity and nurturing energy within yourself. You can focus on creating a warm and comforting environment for yourself and those around you. You may find yourself seeking solace in familiar settings and connecting with loved ones on a deeper, more empathetic level. This lunar transit encourages you to honor your emotions and improve your well-being.

**4 Friday**

The dynamic energy of Mars and Uranus empowers you to take courageous and calculated risks, stepping out of your comfort zone to pursue your passions and aspirations. You can find inventive solutions to challenges and embrace a more authentic expression of yourself. Trust in your ability to navigate the unexpected and seize opportunities for growth and transformation. Embrace the harmonious dance between stability and change, and let your unique brilliance shine.

**5 Saturday**

With Mars forming a trine aspect to Saturn, you may find a harmonious balance between your assertive and disciplined energies. This aspect brings focus, determination, and structure to your endeavors. You will likely experience a strong drive to achieve your goals and the patience and perseverance needed for long-term success. Mars provides motivation and ambition, while Saturn offers the stability and practicality necessary to channel your energy effectively.

**6 Sunday**

Your romantic and social connections infuse passion and harmony, creating a conducive environment for love and cooperation. You can confidently pursue your desires and cultivate healthy and fulfilling relationships. Embrace the joyful and expressive energy of the Moon in Leo, leverage the opportunities presented by the Sun-Jupiter sextile, and nurture the harmonious dynamics of Venus trine Mars to create a fulfilling and rewarding experience in various areas.

**7 Monday**

With Venus conjunct Saturn, you may experience a blend of practicality and seriousness in love, relationships, and personal values. This alignment can bring a sense of commitment and responsibility to your emotional connections, prompting you to approach them with maturity and a desire for long-term stability. This aspect can also highlight the importance of boundaries and realistic expectations in your interactions.

**8 Tuesday**

With Venus in sextile to Uranus, you may experience a delightful blend of excitement and harmony in your relationships and personal values. This aspect encourages you to embrace spontaneity and seek unique experiences that bring joy and fulfillment. Meanwhile, with the Moon's ingress into Virgo, you may notice a heightened sense of practicality and attention to detail in your emotions and daily routines.

**9 Wednesday**

By nurturing the foundations in your life, you cultivate a balanced and stable environment, allowing new leads to emerge and sparking your interest in growth. An opportunity for learning presents itself, serving as a wellspring of inspiration and offering both challenges and opportunities for advancing your career path. An openness to developing your skills increases your life toward greener pastures, ushering in an extended period of growing your dreams.

**10 Thursday**

You seize an enterprising chapter marked by engagement and activity. The fruitful outcome on the horizon enables you to blaze a trail toward rising prospects, promising a time of promise that draws advancement and growth pathways. Working with your talents bears fruit and illuminates a journey that refines your skills. A new vision unfolds as the path shimmers with golden opportunities, ushering in a pivotal time for advancing goals and developing areas of interest.

# APRIL

**11 Friday**

Moon ingress Libra. It's an excellent time to engage in activities that promote peace, beauty, and aesthetic appreciation. Surrounding yourself with art and music or engaging in social gatherings can enhance your well-being and foster a greater sense of connection. Embrace the gentle influence of the Moon in Libra as you navigate the intricacies of human relationships and strive to create a more balanced and harmonious environment for yourself and those around you.

**12 Saturday**

You receive enchanting information promoting harmony and happiness, lighting a path forward for your social life, and you soon find yourself occupied with invitations and get-togethers. Good fortune arrives in a flurry of excitement, ushering in opportunities to mingle. Spending time with companions creates a relaxed environment that nourishes your spirit. You discover the numerous ways you can grow your life as the boundaries of your world expand outwardly.

**13 Sunday**

As the Full Moon graces the celestial sky, you may feel a heightened intensity in your emotional realm. This potent lunar phase illuminates hidden aspects of yourself and invites you to delve deep into your passions, desires, and transformative potential. The Full Moon brings a culmination of energy and a sense of completion, urging you to release what no longer serves you and embrace your natural power.

**14 Monday**

You enter a productive time that offers robust results. Expanding horizons brings a new approach that elevates potential in your career. Life rooms with lighter energy as you chart a course towards a new growth pathway. Being methodical and laying the groundwork enables you to climb the ladder toward a successful outcome in your working life. You are entering a cycle of increasing possibility. You can make the best choices possible for your situation.

**15 Tuesday**

New information cracks the code to a brighter chapter, opening the gate to a fresh start that marks the commencement of a remarkable journey. An area you nurture blossoms into a meaningful path for your social life, connecting you with others on a similar trajectory, willing to support your world with thoughtful discussions and opportunities to mingle. Sharing with valued companions promotes well-being and happiness.

**16 Wednesday**

As the Moon moves into Sagittarius, you may feel a surge of adventurous energy. This cosmic shift encourages you to expand your horizons, seek new experiences, and embrace freedom. Meanwhile, Mercury's ingress into Aries makes your thoughts more spontaneous and action-oriented. You may find yourself enthusiastic and ready to take on new challenges. Trust your intuition, embrace the unknown, and embark on a journey of self-discovery and personal growth.

**17 Thursday**

When Mercury aligns with Neptune in conjunction, it brings a dreamy and imaginative quality to your thoughts and communication. Your mind becomes attuned to nuances and hidden meanings, allowing you to tap into your intuition and connect with the realm of imagination. This cosmic alignment encourages you to trust your inner voice and explore creativity and spirituality. You attract artistic pursuits, seeking inspiration from the ethereal and transcendent.

**18 Friday**

When Mars enters Leo, it ignites a fiery passion, filling you with confidence and courage. You feel driven to pursue goals with enthusiasm and determination, infusing your actions with bold and creative energy. Your self-assurance shines brightly, inspiring others to rally behind your cause and join you. Meanwhile, as the Moon moves into Capricorn, you experience a shift in emotional energy, grounding you and fostering a sense of responsibility and ambition.

**19 Saturday**

As the Sun gracefully enters Taurus, you can embrace a period of stability, grounding, and sensual pleasure. This shift brings a sense of calm and a renewed connection with the natural world. Your focus turns towards the tangible and practical aspects of life, appreciating the simple joys and finding comfort in the material realm. Meanwhile, the harmonious trine between Mars and Neptune enhances your imagination and spiritual sensitivity.

**20 Sunday**

With the Moon's ingress into Aquarius, your emotions attune to the collective, fostering a sense of humanitarianism and a desire for progressive change. You can embrace your unique individuality and contribute to improving the world around you. This Easter Sunday, open yourself to the unexpected, engage in meaningful conversations, and let your heart and mind align in a harmonious dance of growth and enlightenment.

**21 Monday**

In this phase, you encounter a dynamic and potentially challenging energy as the Sun squares Mars. This aspect can bring about a sense of inner tension and a heightened drive for action and assertion. You may desire to assert your will and pursue your goals with great determination. However, it's essential to be mindful of impulsive reactions and potential conflicts. This aspect is a time to harness your energy wisely and channel it into productive and constructive endeavors.

**22 Tuesday**

A productive, busy, and active environment reinforces the improvement of options and offers grounded foundations for a more secure bottom line. This period emphasizes working with your abilities and refining your talents, ultimately placing you in an ideal position for enhancing your career. Being open to new leads is helping you discover a pathway offering promising prospects for your professional life.

**23 Wednesday**

As the Moon ingresses Pisces, you may experience sensitivity and emotional depth. Your intuition amplifies, allowing you to tap into the subtle undercurrents of energy surrounding you. However, the Sun square Pluto aspect brings an intensity to the forefront, stirring the depths of your psyche and challenging you to confront any power struggles or control issues that may arise. This cosmic alignment can be both transformative and challenging.

**24 Thursday**

An idea that you develop soon blossoms into a meaningful venture. This initiative offers an opportunity to work with your abilities and design a path that fosters your talents. As your life expands, optimism increases, encouraging you to reshape your goals actively. You identify viable options that are worth your time, and investing in your skills creates ample room for exploring new interests. These developments usher in a chapter filled with growth.

**25 Friday**

Venus conjunct Saturn. Moon ingress Aries. This combination of energies invites you to balance structure and spontaneity, passion and practicality. It's a time to set clear intentions and assert and pursue desires with a determined yet considerate approach. Trust your instincts, honor your values, and strive for authentic connections that bring stability and excitement. You can navigate gracefully and authentically, paving the way for growth and meaningful relationships.

**26 Saturday**

Your fortune is currently on the upswing, and this is presenting you with the perfect opportunity to embrace a change of pace and engage with a broader world of potential that lies just outside your door. It's also time to connect with friends and increase your involvement in your social life, which bolsters your mood and draws well-being into your world. Thoughtful conversations ahead bring news and information that buoy your spirit, nurturing and renewing your foundations.

**27 Sunday**

With Mars opposing Pluto, you may feel a clash between your willpower and the transformative forces at play. This aspect brings intensity and power struggles, prompting you to confront deep-seated desires and hidden motivations. It's essential to be mindful of power dynamics and avoid engaging in unnecessary conflicts or manipulative behaviors. As the Moon enters Taurus and a New Moon occurs, there is an opportunity for fresh beginnings and grounding energy.

# May

| Sun | Mon | Tue | Wed | Thu | Fri | Sat |
|---|---|---|---|---|---|---|
| | | | | 1 | 2 | 3 |
| 4 | 5 | 6 | 7 | 8 | 9 | 10 |
| 11 | 12 | 13 | 14 | 15 | 16 | 17 |
| 18 | 19 | 20 | 21 | 22 | 23 | 24 |
| 25 | 26 | 27 | 28 | 29 | 30 | 31 |

## NEW MOON

# FLOWER MOON

**28 Monday**

A new project offers excitement and sees the fires of your inspiration burn with creativity. A bustling time of expansion draws well-being as life becomes lighter and more energetic. It provides impressive potential for your life. It lets you establish grounded foundations that promote a balanced environment around your life. Good luck and fortune, and support and nurture your dreams. You turn a corner and head towards a rising possibility.

**29 Tuesday**

When the Moon ingresses Gemini, you may embrace curiosity and heightened mental agility. Your mind becomes more adaptable and receptive to new ideas, allowing you to engage in lively conversations and explore various interests. This period encourages you to express yourself more efficiently and connect with others through meaningful dialogue. You may find yourself seeking intellectual stimulation and pursuing diverse sources of information.

**30 Wednesday**

Venus ingress Aries. This transit encourages you to express your individuality and pursue your passions with confidence and vigor. Embrace the courage to go after what you want, and don't be afraid to assert your needs in your relationships. It is a time to explore your desires, cultivate self-love, and embrace the power of your magnetism. Allow Venus in Aries to inspire you to express yourself and pursue your heart's desires boldly.

**1 Thursday**

As the Moon ingresses into Cancer, you may notice a shift in your emotional landscape. Cancer is a sensitive and nurturing sign, and its influence can bring forth a deep sense of empathy and intuition within you. You may find yourself more attuned to your emotions and those around you. Prioritize self-care and create a nurturing environment for yourself and your loved ones. You may desire to connect with your family or establish a sense of security in your home.

# MAY

**2 Friday**

When Venus and Neptune unite, you immerse in enchantment and heightened ideals. This celestial alignment sparks a deep sense of compassion, empathy, and sensitivity in your interactions and relationships. You may experience a strong desire for connection and spiritual union, seeking to transcend the boundaries of everyday reality. Your artistic and creative expression may also flourish under this influence as you tap into the ethereal realms of imagination and beauty.

**3 Saturday**

When the Moon enters Leo, you may feel confident and self-assuredness. It is a time to embrace your inner lion and let your unique qualities shine brightly. You might seek attention, admiration, and applause. It's a beautiful opportunity to express your creativity and passion and to engage in activities that ignite your enthusiasm. Your emotions may become more dramatic and expressive, and you may find yourself craving affection and appreciation from others.

**4 Sunday**

When Pluto turns retrograde, you may experience a profound internal shift that invites you to delve deep into the depths of your psyche. This planetary event urges you to confront your shadow self, face your fears, and explore the hidden recesses of your subconscious mind. It's a time of introspection and transformation, where you can release old patterns, beliefs, and attachments that no longer serve your growth.

## 5 Monday

With the Moon's ingress into Virgo, you feel a practical and analytical approach to your emotions and daily activities. It's a time to pay attention to details, organize your thoughts, and establish order. This combination of Mercury sextile Jupiter and the Moon in Virgo supports you in expanding your knowledge, refining your skills, and bringing clarity and efficiency to your endeavors. Embrace the energy of growth, learning, and practicality surrounding you.

## 6 Tuesday

When Venus forms a sextile aspect with Pluto, you may experience a powerful and transformative influence on your relationships and personal values. This harmonious alignment encourages deep emotional connections and the potential for profound experiences in love and intimacy. Your desires and passions intensify, and you may feel drawn to explore the depths of your emotions and the hidden aspects of your relationships.

## 7 Wednesday

A lucky break brings a valuable opportunity that feeds your soul, benefiting your life on several levels as energy improves and you feel more happy and optimistic about the potential possible in your world. An endeavor you develop progresses and keeps life humming along as you engage in projects and areas that capture your inspiration. Your ability to work towards a plan produces an abundant harvest that enriches your life.

## 8 Thursday

Moon ingress Libra. You desire to connect with others intellectually and emotionally, seeking companionship and cooperation. This transit invites you to explore the art of compromise and finding common ground in your relationships. It's a time to cultivate grace, charm, and diplomacy as you navigate the intricacies of human connections. Allow the gentle influence of the Moon in Libra to guide you in creating harmonious relationships and fostering inner and outer balance.

# May

**9 Friday**

Information arrives that shines a light on unique goals, increasing freedom and adventure on the horizon, tempting you towards lush green pastures. The seeds planted during this time blossom into a happy journey towards growing life. Adding fuel to motivation sees inspiration skyrocket, fanning the flames of your creativity and giving you a chance to discover pathways that nurture your capabilities. Growing your talents in a new area opens the gate to transformation.

---

**10 Saturday**

Mercury ingress Taurus. Moon ingress Scorpio. You might explore the depths of your inner world, seeking emotional authenticity and a deeper understanding of your desires and motivations. This combination of Mercury in Taurus and the Moon in Scorpio invites you to engage in meaningful conversations and delve into the mysteries of your psyche. It's a time for thoughtful reflection and insightful exchanges, allowing you to uncover hidden truths and make grounded decisions.

---

**11 Sunday**

From heartfelt cards to thoughtful gifts, spending quality time together, or simply sharing kind words, Mother's Day allows us to make these extraordinary women feel cherished and valued. In a world that can sometimes be challenging, mothers and mother figures stand as beacons of love and strength, and on this day, we have the chance to shine a light on their importance. Happy Mother's Day to all the incredible moms and mother figures out there! 🌼 💖 👩‍👧‍👦

---

**12 Monday**

During the Full Moon, the intensity of emotions peaks, illuminating areas of your life that require attention and transformation. This lunar phase brings a heightened sense of awareness and a powerful surge of energy. With Mercury square Pluto, there is a potential for profound insights to emerge through intense conversations and self-reflection. You may find yourself delving into the depths of your thoughts and uncovering hidden truths.

**13 Tuesday**

As the Moon enters Sagittarius, you may feel a sense of expansion and a desire for adventure. This transit encourages you to explore new horizons, both internally and externally. A quest for knowledge, truth, and higher meaning may ignite your emotions. It can broaden your perspectives as you seek new experiences and embrace an optimistic and adventurous outlook. You may explore different belief systems and engage in activities that nourish your spirit.

**14 Wednesday**

You have an opportunity to develop an area that offers improvement, working on your goals to see an influx of favorable signs that let you know you can create progress if you focus on achieving your best. Planning and tweaking projects offer rising results, bringing valuable rewards flowing into your life. Your willingness to be adaptable and pivot at a moment's notice will come in handy when surprise news lands in your lap.

**15 Thursday**

As the Moon enters Capricorn, you may notice a shift in your emotional landscape. Capricorn brings a sense of groundedness and practicality to your emotions, encouraging you to approach life with a structured and disciplined mindset. You may focus on your long-term goals and ambitions, feeling motivated to work hard and progress. You may be more attuned to your responsibilities and commitments, seeking stability and reliability in your actions.

**16 Friday**

Being open to new people and possibilities brings a top result to your social life, leaving the drama behind as you turn a new page in your book of life. Changes ahead bring a high note into your life, ruling a time of sharing companionship with people who get a boost into your world. Expanding your circle of friends helps you connect with others who support your personal growth and evolution, setting the tone for a prosperous path that brings a sweet flavor into your life.

**17 Saturday**

When the Sun aligns with Uranus in conjunction, you may experience a burst of energy and a strong desire for freedom and change. Embrace the significance of innovation and let your creative ideas flow freely. Be open to new perspectives and possibilities that come your way. Remember to stay grounded amidst the excitement and balance your need for freedom and responsibilities. Trust in your ability to navigate the unexpected and embrace life's surprises.

**18 Sunday**

With the Moon entering Aquarius, you're encouraged to approach situations more detached and rationally. This cosmic combination invites you to step back and observe your emotions and thoughts with a greater sense of objectivity. It's a time to embrace innovation and open-mindedness, seeking unique solutions to challenges. It's a time to embrace progressive thinking, innovative solutions, and the power of collaboration.

**19 Monday**

Any projects you initiate soon offer room to grow your talents, with your practical and creative abilities ready to nurture expansion in your life. Against a bountiful backdrop of rising confidence and refreshing opportunities, it gives you a chance to refine your skills and grow your abilities. Exploring a variety of techniques offers refinement and advances your skills, focusing on developing your career path to merge your aspirations with tangible results.

**20 Tuesday**

As the Sun moves into Gemini, your energy may shift towards curiosity, adaptability, and social engagement. You may feel more intellectually stimulated and eager to learn new things. It's a time to embrace versatility and expand your horizons through communication and networking. This energy encourages you to strike a balance between practicality and imagination, grounding yourself while also embracing the diversity of experiences and ideas that come your way.

**21 Wednesday**

Dedication and perseverance help you turn a corner and enter a winning streak as a time of blossoming activity begins a journey filled with hope and promise. You cast your net wide and discover pleasing results, upgrading your skills that crack the code to rising prospects in your career path. An emphasis on improving your life creates a bridge towards a more secure future, helping you launch into a progressive chapter of developing plans.

**22 Thursday**

When Venus forms a harmonious trine aspect with Mars, it balances passion and harmony in your relationships and personal desires. This aspect encourages you to pursue your desires with confidence, assertiveness, and a healthy dose of charm. Your values fuel your actions, and you are more attuned to the needs and desires of others. The Sun's sextile aspect to Neptune enhances your intuition, creativity, and spiritual awareness.

### 23 Friday

A new approach brings the correct result into your life, seeding meaningful conversations that offer collaboration and a creative boost. It provides a chance to switch lanes and develop artistic goals, reshuffling the decks of potential as it broadens your circle of friends and puts you in contact with like-minded people who offer support and social engagement. An experimental attitude draws new pathways into your life and helps you capitalize on the potential surrounding you.

### 24 Saturday

When the Sun forms a harmonious trine aspect with Pluto, you can tap into your personal power and transformational energy. This aspect empowers you to make positive changes in your life, embracing your inner strength and resilience. You may feel a deep sense of purpose and determination, allowing you to overcome obstacles and achieve your goals confidently. With the Moon entering Taurus, you are grounded and focused on stability and material matters.

### 25 Sunday

When Saturn enters Aries, it significantly shifts your life's lessons and challenges. This transit calls for a disciplined and responsible approach to asserting yourself and pursuing your goals. Saturn's presence in Aries urges you to take charge of your ambitions and work diligently towards achieving them. It brings a sense of structure and discipline to your actions, pushing you to overcome obstacles and develop a strong sense of self-reliance.

**26 Monday**

As Mercury enters Gemini, your communication skills and mental agility heighten. With Mercury sextile Saturn, you can apply a practical and disciplined approach to your thinking and communication. Your ideas are well-structured, and you possess the focus and determination to see them through. As the Moon enters Gemini, your emotional state aligns with your mental processes, allowing you to express your feelings and thoughts with clarity and coherence.

**27 Tuesday**

During the New Moon, a potent energy of fresh beginnings and new possibilities fills the air. It's a time when you can set intentions and plant the seeds of your desires for the upcoming lunar cycle. With Mercury trine Pluto, your mind delves deeper insights and profound transformations. This aspect empowers you to delve into the depths of your psyche, uncover hidden truths, and communicate authentically. You can penetrate beneath the surface with clarity and precision.

**28 Wednesday**

You may draw nurturing and emotional connections as the Moon moves into Cancer. This transit is a time to honor and embrace your feelings, allowing them to guide you toward a deeper understanding of yourself and others. Your intuition and sensitivity heighten, offering valuable insights into your emotional landscape. Creating a safe and supportive environment where you can express and process your emotions is essential.

**29 Thursday**

You enter a time of rising prospects that crack the code to growing your world, emphasizing a transformational journey that harmonizes your spirit and soothes restlessness, bringing a pursuit that captures your interest. It is a wise investment as it draws dividends into your life, channeling your resources, seeing life brimming with potential, with a favorable opportunity that comes along to help you promote growth and advancement.

# JUNE

| Sun | Mon | Tue | Wed | Thu | Fri | Sat |
|---|---|---|---|---|---|---|
| 1 | 2 | 3 | 4 | 5 | 6 | 7 |
| 8 | 9 | 10 | 11 | 12 | 13 | 14 |
| 15 | 16 | 17 | 18 | 19 | 20 | 21 |
| 22 | 23 | 24 | 25 | 26 | 27 | 28 |
| 29 | 30 | | | | | |

## New Moon

# STRAWBERRY MOON

**30 Friday**

As the Sun and Mercury align, there is a powerful fusion of self-expression and intellectual clarity within you. Your thoughts and communication are infused with a vibrant energy, allowing you to articulate your ideas confidently and passionately. With the Moon moving into Leo, you are encouraged to shine your light brightly and embrace your unique creativity. This ingress is a time to let your authentic self shine as you enthusiastically share your passions and aspirations.

**31 Saturday**

Life is ripe with potential, ready to blossom as you breeze through an ample time of discovering new possibilities in sync with expanding life and growing your world in a new direction. Complications fade away as sunny skies loom overhead, with unexpected news bringing a busy time filled with the promise of a brighter future. You settle into a productive groove that grows into a meaningful path forward.

**1 Sunday**

The feeling of being in limbo soon shifts as news arrives offering expansion. You no longer need to sit tight as fantastic opportunities set the stage for golden moments shared with friends. Engaging with your broader circle of companions brings an event or trip to look forward to, delivering a happy surprise to your life. Reconnecting with friends warms your heart, sharing ideas and thoughts that boost your well-being and reveal new possibilities in projects and friendships.

## JUNE

### 2 Monday

As the Moon enters Virgo, you may find yourself attuned to detail and focused on practical matters. It is a time to embrace your analytical nature and pay attention to the small things contributing to your overall well-being. Your organizational skills and ability to discern what needs improvement rise. It's an excellent time to prioritize self-care, streamline your daily routines, and create a sense of order in your environment.

### 3 Tuesday

Researching various options helps you develop a winning trajectory, drawing a lighter path that offers a learning curve you find fascinating. A new role grows your skills, and your attention to detail and meticulous approach develop your talents, bringing a productive chapter that heightens security in your life. Gaining traction on your working goals helps you create substantial gains that improve your day-to-day life.

### 4 Wednesday

As the Moon moves into Libra, you may find yourself naturally inclined towards harmony, balance, and cooperation in your interactions. This transit is a time to prioritize diplomacy and seek compromises to maintain peaceful relationships. You may feel a sense of social awareness, seeking to create a pleasant and harmonious atmosphere in your interactions. Your focus may shift towards finding common ground and understanding different perspectives.

### 5 Thursday

With Venus sextile Jupiter, you experience a boost of optimism and expansiveness. This aspect brings a harmonious blend of love, abundance, and good fortune. You feel open to opportunities for growth and enjoyment. It's a time to embrace the beauty of life, indulge in pleasurable experiences, and connect with others on a deeper level. Additionally, with Mercury sextile Mars, you have the potential to enhance your communication and mental agility.

**6 Friday**

Venus slips into Taurus, bringing sensual and earthy energy. This transit invites you to embrace and appreciate the beauty and pleasures surrounding you. You may find yourself drawn to activities and experiences that engage your senses, such as indulging in delicious food, surrounding yourself with soothing aesthetics, or taking time to luxuriate in self-care. This ingress is a time to cultivate a more profound sense of self and to nurture your relationships with love and tenderness.

**7 Saturday**

When the Moon ingresses Scorpio, you may experience intense emotions and a sense of introspection. This transit encourages you to delve into the depths of your psyche, uncovering hidden truths and understanding the complexities of your feelings. You may seek meaningful connections and crave emotional depth in your interactions. This transit is a time of transformation and regeneration, where you can confront and release any emotional baggage that no longer serves you.

**8 Sunday**

When Mercury conjuncts Jupiter and ingresses Cancer, you may feel a surge of expansive and nurturing energy in your communication and thought processes. This alignment amplifies your ability to express yourself with wisdom, optimism, and emotional sensitivity, allowing you to communicate and connect with others profoundly. It is a time of seeking knowledge and expanding your intellectual horizons, particularly in areas related to emotions, home, and family.

### 9 Monday

When Mercury squares Saturn, you may experience challenges and limitations in your communication and thinking processes. It's essential to be cautious, as misunderstandings and delays are possible. However, this aspect also offers an opportunity for practical thinking and disciplined focus. As the Moon enters Sagittarius, emotions heighten, and you're inclined to seek adventure. It's a time to expand your horizons, explore ideas, and embrace a sense of optimism.

### 10 Tuesday

Information arrives that opens the gate to an uptick of potential, bringing new pathways that offer growth as you get a glimpse of a prestigious area that comes calling to advance life forward. It brings encouragement that helps you grow your life in a unique direction, with positive results that help you feel confident and ready to tackle new goals with enthusiasm. Acting on instincts lets you spot a diamond in the rough, as this sideline project advances your knowledge base.

### 11 Wednesday

This particular Full Moon brings the harmonious aspect of Mercury sextile Venus, enhancing your communication skills and social interactions. You will likely express yourself with grace and charm, making connecting and building cooperative relationships easier. This alignment fosters creativity, diplomacy, and cooperation, allowing you to find common ground and create mutually beneficial connections.

### 12 Thursday

As the Moon enters Capricorn, a grounded and practical energy envelops your being. This lunar transit lets you focus on your responsibilities, ambitions, and long-term goals. You may find yourself drawn to tasks that require discipline, organization, and a strategic approach. The Moon in Capricorn encourages you to take a structured and systematic approach to achieve your objectives. Use this time to assess your priorities, make practical decisions, and lay a solid foundation.

**13 Friday**

This seemingly ominous day combines the superstitions surrounding both Fridays and the number 13. Whether you're superstitious or not, Friday the 13th can be an opportunity to reflect on the power of belief and how it shapes our perceptions. It's a reminder that the significance of a day is what we make of it and that our beliefs can influence our experiences. So, on this Friday, the 13th, you can choose to embrace it with a sense of curiosity and see where the day takes you.

**14 Saturday**

Moon ingress Aquarius is a time to embrace your uniqueness and celebrate your individuality. Allow yourself to think outside the box, challenge the status quo, and pursue intellectual pursuits that ignite your curiosity. The Moon in Aquarius encourages you to connect with your community and contribute to causes that align with your values. It's a time to embrace authenticity, honor your intellectual needs, and nurture your well-being by belonging to a tribe of like-minded souls.

**15 Sunday**

When Mars squares Uranus and Jupiter squares Saturn, you may experience a tension between your desire for change and your need for stability. The energy can feel intense and unpredictable, causing a clash between your assertiveness and the limitations or restrictions in your life. It's essential to be cautious and mindful of impulsive actions or rebellious tendencies during this time. Find a balance between taking risks and considering the potential consequences.

**16 Monday**

Moon ingress Pisces. Trust your intuition and allow your imagination to guide you. This period invites introspection, creative expression, and interconnectedness with the universe. Embrace the gentle and ethereal energy of Pisces. Let it inspire you to tap into your intuition, find solace in introspection, and connect with the deeper aspects of yourself. Embrace the healing energy of Pisces and allow it to guide a journey of self-discovery and emotional fulfillment.

**17 Tuesday**

Mars ingress Virgo. Paying attention to the small steps and being meticulous in your approach can yield significant results. Use this period to harness your determination, discipline, and analytical skills to make progress. Remember to balance your drive with self-care and flexibility, as Mars in Virgo can sometimes bring a tendency to be perfectionistic. Trust in your ability to bring order and efficiency to your endeavors, and enjoy the satisfaction of a job well done.

**18 Wednesday**

Moon ingress Aries. Aries is a fiery and assertive sign known for its boldness and passion. You can take the lead, embrace beginnings, and assert your individuality during this time. You may feel more courageous and confident in pursuing your goals and expressing your needs. It's a favorable period for taking action, initiating projects, and pushing forward with determination. Use this time to ignite your passions, embrace your inner strength, and fearlessly pursue your desires.

**19 Thursday**

When Jupiter squares Neptune, you may face a challenge between idealism and reality. This aspect can bring about a sense of confusion or uncertainty regarding your beliefs and aspirations. You might feel torn between your desire for expansion and growth (Jupiter) and the need to confront the truth and be grounded (Neptune). It's important to stay grounded and realistic in your expectations while remaining open to the possibilities that arise.

**20 Friday**

Change is imminent and brings a boost into your life, offering an upgrade that fosters expansion and progress, eliminating restrictions as you crack the code to a brighter chapter. It fuels your motivation and inspiration while a flood of new options expands your world, providing an opportunity to explore new leads that bring rising prospects. It opens a path that dispels heaviness and leads to an enterprising time for planning and researching potential options.

**21 Saturday**

The June Solstice marks the beginning of a new season, inviting you to reflect on your goals, dreams, and aspirations. It's a time to set intentions and embrace the energy of growth and renewal. Use this period to establish a solid foundation and cultivate a sense of emotional security. By aligning yourself with the natural rhythms of the season, you can tap into the transformative power of the solstice and embark on a journey of self-discovery and personal growth.

**22 Sunday**

With Mars forming a harmonious sextile to Jupiter and the Sun squaring Saturn, you find yourself in a dynamic and challenging period of growth and expansion. The Mars-Jupiter sextile brings enthusiasm, confidence, and motivation to pursue your goals and take bold actions. It's a time to embrace opportunities, explore new territories, and push beyond your comfort zone. However, the Sun's square to Saturn introduces a dose of reality and potential obstacles along the way.

**23 Monday**

With the Moon shifting into Gemini, your emotional focus is curiosity, communication, and intellectual pursuits. You feel a need for mental stimulation and variety in your daily experiences. However, be aware of the Sun's square aspect to Neptune, which can create a sense of confusion or uncertainty in your perception of reality. It's important to stay grounded and discerning, as Neptune's influence can blur boundaries and make it hard to see clearly.

**24 Tuesday**

When the Sun aligns with Jupiter in conjunction, it signifies a time of expansion, abundance, and optimism in your life. You experience a boost of confidence, enthusiasm, and a sense of purpose. Opportunities for growth and success may present themselves, and you are encouraged to seize them enthusiastically. This alignment also highlights the importance of broadening your horizons through travel, education, or exploring new philosophies and beliefs.

**25 Wednesday**

The New Moon in Cancer provides a nurturing and supportive environment for self-reflection, healing, and setting intentions that align with your heart's desires. Use this time to create a vision for the future, cultivate self-care practices, and foster meaningful connections with loved ones. By honoring your emotions and embracing the energy of the New Moon, you can embark on a journey of personal growth and create a life that resonates with your deepest needs and desires.

**26 Thursday**

As Mercury moves into Leo, your communication style becomes more confident and bold. You are ready to share your ideas and take the stage. Embrace this energy to express yourself authentically and fearlessly. Allow your passion to shine and let your creative spark ignite new opportunities and connections. Trust in your ability to communicate with clarity and conviction, and let your voice lead. You can captivate others with your words and make a lasting impression.

**27 Friday**

With the Moon shifting into Leo, you can embrace your inner light and express your unique essence. Leo energy encourages you to enter the spotlight, share your talents, and confidently radiate your authentic self. This transit is a time to embrace self-expression, creativity, and passion. Allow your creative juices to flow freely and fearlessly as you tap into your creative potential and shine your light on the world.

**28 Saturday**

Mercury trine Saturn is when your mind is sharp and focused, allowing you to approach tasks and challenges clearly and efficiently. Your thoughts are grounded and structured, enabling you to make well-informed decisions and communicate effectively. At the same time, the trine to Neptune infuses your thinking with inspiration and intuition. You can tap into your imagination and access more profound levels of understanding.

**29 Sunday**

Mercury opposed Pluto. This opposition can bring about deep introspection and a desire to uncover hidden truths and secrets. Your mind may delve into complex and sensitive subjects, leading to intense conversations and inner turmoil. Maintaining a balanced perspective and avoiding being overwhelmed by power struggles or obsessive thinking is essential. The Moon's ingress into Virgo brings a more practical and detail-oriented energy, urging you to focus on the present.

## <u>July</u>

| Sun | Mon | Tue | Wed | Thu | Fri | Sat |
|---|---|---|---|---|---|---|
| | | 1 | 2  | 3 | 4 | 5 |
| 6 | 7 | 8 | 9 | 10 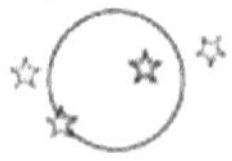 | 11 | 12 |
| 13 | 14 | 15 | 16 | 17 | 18  | 19 |
| 20 | 21 | 22 | 23 | 24  | 25 | 26 |
| 27 | 28 | 29 | 30 | 31 | | |

LEO

## New Moon

## BUCK MOON

**30 Monday**

Staying flexible and adaptable helps you pivot towards new possibilities that crop up, bringing an extensive chapter of moving into uncharted territory. A buzz of excitement brings new options that hit a sweet note in your life as you discover circumstances become more stable and grounded. You're heading towards a sound chapter of growth and progression, creating a shift that offers purpose and productivity.

**1 Tuesday**

When the Moon enters Libra, you may feel a heightened sense of harmony, balance, and a desire for peace in your emotional world. You find yourself seeking fairness and understanding in your interactions with others. The Libra Moon encourages you to consider different perspectives and find common ground in conflicts. It brings a gentle and diplomatic energy that promotes cooperation and cooperation in your relationships.

**2 Wednesday**

Exploring options for development sparks an emotional journey that expands your vision in a new direction, connecting with information that arrives in a flurry of excitement. A large part of this news centers on self-development and prioritizing your goals, leading you to a lucrative avenue offering rising prospects and a secure foundation for growing your world. Life aligns with your dreams and hopes as you merge them with the rising tide of refreshing options.

**3 Thursday**

Information arrives bearing positive news, offering an element of surprise instrumental in increasing luck and providing you with rising prospects. It emphasizes your social and home life, bestowing happy news and opportunities for developing friendships. It ushers in improvement into your social life. It brings a chance to mingle with friends, sparking lively discussions that nurture creativity and fresh ideas, opening the floodgates to a chapter of growth and well-being.

**4 Friday**

When the Moon moves into Scorpio, you may experience emotional intensity and desire profound transformation. This astrological transit brings forth the need to delve into the depths of your emotions and explore the mysteries of your inner world. The Scorpio Moon invites you to embrace vulnerability's transformative power and confront hidden truths or unresolved feelings. It's a time of emotional healing and rebirth, allowing you to release and make way for new beginnings.

**5 Saturday**

Increasing activity in your social life brings unexpected invitations to mingle, promoting thoughtful discussions with a diverse group of people who nurture companionship. Expanding your circle of friends attracts good luck, opening the portal to social engagement that supports well-being. It ushers in an upbeat time of lively discussions, fostering a stable foundation for expanding your life in a favorable direction.

**6 Sunday**

When Venus forms a sextile aspect with Saturn, it brings a harmonious and stabilizing influence. As the Moon enters Sagittarius, you feel renewed adventure and enthusiasm. Your emotions lift, and you crave exploring new horizons. It's a time to embrace the freedom to learn, grow, and expand your worldview. Trust your instincts, follow your passions, and allow the energy of these celestial influences to guide you on a journey of discovery and fulfillment.

**7 Monday**

With Uranus in Gemini and Venus trine Pluto, you are encouraged to embrace change, embrace your unique expression, and nurture transformative connections. It is a powerful time for personal growth, self-discovery, and creating profound shifts in your relationships and overall life path. Trust the process and embrace the opportunities that come your way, as they hold the potential to revolutionize your world and lead to meaningful and transformative experiences.

**8 Tuesday**

A new opportunity emerges, setting your life in motion and acting as a breath of fresh air, doubling your luck and good fortune. Energizing information spotlights your creativity and encourages you to share your abilities with a broader audience, connecting you with like-minded people ready to engage in discussions and collaborations. A change of scene helps you move toward expanding your life in a prosperous direction, increasing the pace and offering growth and progression.

**9 Wednesday**

With the Moon entering Capricorn, you may find yourself drawn towards a more focused and disciplined approach in various areas of your life. This transit brings a sense of practicality and a desire to work diligently towards your goals. You will likely feel more grounded and responsible, ready to tackle challenges with determination and perseverance. It is a favorable time to prioritize your long-term aspirations and take steps toward materializing them.

**10 Thursday**

During a Full Moon, you may experience heightened emotions and awareness. It's a time of culmination and completion, where the energy is potent, and emotions may run deep. You might reflect on your progress, celebrate achievements, or evaluate areas of your life that need attention. This cosmic aspect is a powerful time to release what no longer serves you and let go of any emotional baggage.

**11 Friday**

Moon ingress Aquarius. You may feel inspired to break free from conventional norms and explore new and innovative ideas. Embrace your eccentricities and allow your creativity to flow. Connect with like-minded individuals who share your vision and values. Use this time to cultivate friendships and collaborations that support your growth and bring positive change to the world around you. Embrace the progressive energy of Aquarius and let your inner rebel shine.

**12 Saturday**

A touch of magic infuses your life with a sparkling aura of positivity. Optimism abounds as you shed the burden of stress and engage in heartfelt exchanges with friends and family. Life's rhythm settles into a more manageable tempo, introducing enhanced stability to your surroundings. Cultivating well-balanced foundations paves the way for a solid platform from which to expand your world. Formulating plans and expectations empowers you to craft a vision for growth.

**13 Sunday**

Saturn turns retrograde—Moon ingress Pisces. You may find yourself dreamy and reflective, seeking solace and connection to your inner world. You may engage in creative and spiritual practices and nurture your emotional well-being. Take the opportunity to dive deep into your subconscious and explore the hidden realms of your psyche. Use this reflection and dynamic sensitivity period to gain insights, release what no longer serves you, and realign yourself with your soul's path.

**14 Monday**

New opportunities emerge, prompting you to contemplate growth, learning, and advancement. The prospect of a course or other learning opportunity serves as a wellspring of inspiration, dismantling barriers and guiding you toward growth. While challenges lie ahead, they promise progression and enrichment for your life. Embracing change ushers you toward greener pastures, inviting a journey of self-development and a fruitful period of growing dreams.

**15 Tuesday**

Harmonizing your vision for future growth amplifies the rewards in your career path. Information you uncover becomes a catalyst for exceptional progress. Well-crafted ideas prepare for launch, enabling you to refine your skills and remaining open to supplementary options aids in establishing unique goals that empower your abilities. Through research and planning, you can delineate potential areas for development. Life offers a multifaceted spectrum of intriguing leads.

**16 Wednesday**

Moon ingress Aries. This fiery energy can inspire you to be more confident, courageous, and decisive in your choices. Trust your instincts and follow your passions; this is a time of self-discovery and empowerment. Embrace the spirit of adventure and embrace the opportunities that come your way. Let the Moon in Aries ignite your inner spark and propel you toward personal growth and achievement.

**17 Thursday**

Anticipate a turning point in your life where openness to change and possibility releases you from restrictive patterns that have held you back. Self-discovery and personal growth take center stage as you steer your course toward nurturing a meaningful domain that breathes fresh vitality into your life. Creativity soars as you discover new information, leading you into a realm of learning and kindling your inspiration ushers in a busy period where you put your talents to work.

**18 Friday**

As Mercury turns retrograde, you may experience a shift in your communication and thought processes. It's a time to slow down, reflect, and reconsider your plans and ideas. Take the opportunity to review and revise any essential decisions or projects. With the Moon entering Taurus, you may feel a grounding and stabilizing influence in your emotions and surroundings. It's a favorable time to focus on practical matters and establish security and stability in your life.

**19 Saturday**

An upcoming shift in pace and environment ushers in a brighter chapter, fueling your optimism about the potential that exists in your world. Your creativity and inspiration shine brightly, revealing a treasure trove of potential pathways. It marks a time of strategic planning and cultivating your dreams and aspirations, where enriching conversations with thoughtful companions nurture your well-being and lead to increased happiness in your social life.

**20 Sunday**

Your mind is agile and adaptable, allowing you to grasp information quickly and connect with different concepts. It's a favorable period for learning, sharing ideas, and expanding your knowledge. Embrace the lightness and playfulness of Gemini Moon energy as you explore interests and engage in stimulating activities. Stay open to new perspectives and be willing to embrace the duality of life. Use this time to nourish curiosity and foster connections that enrich your mind and spirit.

**21 Monday**

Well-crafted ideas get a chance to shine, underscoring the essence of manifestation and magic, helping you create remarkable progress, gaining traction on developing your vision, and entering a cycle of increasing possibility. It enables you to set sail on a timely voyage that offers ample room to reinvent your skills in an industry that feels like the right fit for your talents. Reshuffling the decks of potential brings a unique path to your life.

**22 Tuesday**

It's a time to tune into your feelings and nurture yourself and those around you. Let your heart guide you as you embrace your passions and take center stage. Allow the nurturing energy of Cancer Moon and the confident energy of Leo to blend harmoniously, supporting you in expressing your authentic essence and cultivating joy in your relationships and endeavors. Embrace this time of emotional abundance, self-expression, and heartfelt connections.

**23 Wednesday**

As the Sun forms a harmonious sextile with Uranus, you may experience an exciting burst of energy and a desire for change and innovation. This aspect encourages you to embrace your individuality and express yourself authentically. You may feel inspired to break free from old patterns and explore new possibilities in your life. Meanwhile, the square between Venus and Mars creates a dynamic tension between your desires and actions.

**24 Thursday**

The Sun trine Neptune adds a touch of magic and inspiration to the mix. It invites you to tap into your intuition and dream big, allowing your imagination to guide you toward new possibilities. The New Moon marks a fresh start, a time to set intentions and plant the seeds for future growth. It's an opportunity to align your desires with your actions and embark on a journey of self-discovery and manifestation.

**25 Friday**

You may experience power dynamics and transformative energies when the Sun opposes Pluto. This aspect challenges you to confront deep-seated fears, desires, and control issues. It's a time of personal growth and evolution, where you are encouraged to delve into the depths of your being and confront any hidden aspects of yourself. This opposition can bring internal and external struggles, but it also offers an opportunity for transformation.

**26 Saturday**

When the Moon ingresses Virgo, you feel an inclination to focus on practical matters and details. You are likely to have a heightened sense of organization, efficiency, and attention to cleanliness. You may find yourself analyzing and refining your routines, seeking ways to improve productivity and create a sense of order in your daily activities. This influence can also bring a desire for self-improvement and a willingness to work diligently toward your goals.

**27 Sunday**

An open road of potential is about to unfold before you, beckoning you to explore. Embracing new people and possibilities will nurture your life. This journey marks the beginning of an active chapter that invites you to engage with a broader world of potential in your social life. Opportunities are knocking, helping you to turn the page to a fresh cycle of growth. Navigating an ever-changing environment with flexibility and adaptability lays the foundations from which to grow your world.

**28 Monday**

Hidden pathways become visible, revealing intriguing options for your life. You create a bridge leading to greener pastures, marking the inception of expanding your world. This busy period invites you to launch your talents to new heights, fostering an active environment that connects you with kindred spirits who share common interests and creativity. Refining your talents and creative skills opens the floodgates to rising potential in your life.

**29 Tuesday**

You might feel more empathetic and understanding toward others' perspectives. This period can also inspire you to create a harmonious and aesthetically pleasing environment in your home or workspace. Embrace the energy of Libra's peaceful and diplomatic nature, and use it to foster positive connections and find common ground with those around you. Embrace the Libra Moon energy to cultivate fairness, diplomacy, and a sense of mutual respect in your interactions.

**30 Wednesday**

Change encompasses your world, ushering in progress that empowers you to pursue a long-held dream. It brings a breakthrough that sparks fresh possibilities and options. The path ahead suddenly opens up, leading you in a curious direction for personal development. It unveils unique options, fostering an enterprising avenue forward and providing a productive chapter dedicated to achieving your goals. Ambition surges, energizing a chapter that inspires and motivates growth.

**31 Thursday**

With Venus entering Cancer, you may seek emotional connection and comfort in your relationships. During this time, you might desire to nurture and care for your loved ones and prioritize creating a sense of security and stability in your home and personal life. This transit can deepen your emotional bonds and enhance your ability to express your feelings to others. With the Moon in Scorpio, your emotions may intensify, leading to understanding your desires and motivations.

# AUGUST

| Sun | Mon | Tue | Wed | Thu | Fri | Sat |
|---|---|---|---|---|---|---|
| | | | | | 1  | 2 |
| 3 | 4 | 5 | 6 | 7 | 8 | 9 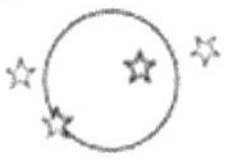 |
| 10 | 11 | 12 | 13 | 14 | 15 | 16  |
| 17 | 18 | 19 | 20 | 21 | 22 | 23  |
| 24 | 25 | 26 | 27 | 28 | 29 | 30 |
| 31  | | | | | | |

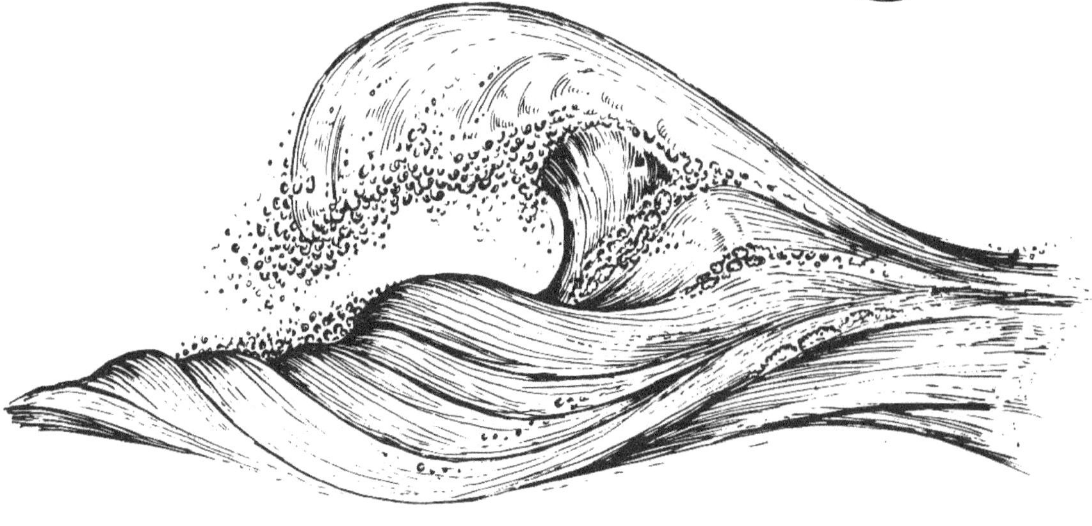

## New Moon

## STURGEON MOON

# AUGUST

## 1 Friday

Venus square Saturn. Venus square Neptune. You may experience a temporary lack of clarity in your romantic pursuits or find it difficult to discern between genuine connections and illusions. Use this period to reflect on your values and boundaries in relationships, and take the time to address any underlying issues that may be surfacing. Acknowledging and working through these challenges can foster more robust and authentic connections with others in the long run.

## 2 Saturday

New information arrives, shedding light on a fresh possibility. Transformations in your wider social environment help leave behind any lingering issues and drama. It sets the stage for an exciting chapter filled with lively discussions and thoughtful dialogues, imbuing your life with a sense of adventure and freedom. You connect with kindred spirits and enjoy some well-deserved downtime, rejuvenating your emotional reserves and laying the groundwork for a new chapter in your life.

## 3 Sunday

As the Moon enters Sagittarius, you may feel a sense of adventure and optimism sweeping over you. This planetary shift encourages you to seek new experiences, expand your horizons, and embrace a more adventurous spirit. Your curiosity may be piqued, urging you to explore different philosophies, cultures, or belief systems. This transit is a favorable time to engage in activities that challenge your intellect and provide opportunities for personal growth.

# AUGUST

## 4 Monday

New options ahead bring a whirlwind of activity into your life, fostering a bustling environment that grows your talents and nurtures your abilities. Launching an area for development yields tangible results and brings advancement to your career path, ensuring a steady progression in your working life. It opens a lucrative path that draws rising prospects into your life, where being resourceful and researching new options bring results that pave the way for advancement.

## 5 Tuesday

As the Moon enters Capricorn, you may feel more focused, disciplined, and determined. This transit brings a sense of practicality and a desire to achieve your goals. You might notice a shift in emotions towards a more responsible outlook. It's a time to set intentions and work diligently toward them. The Capricorn influence encourages you to take charge of your life and responsibilities, reminding you of the importance of staying grounded and organized.

## 6 Wednesday

As Mars enters Libra, you may experience a shift in your energy and approach to relationships and conflicts. This transit encourages you to seek harmony and balance in your interactions. You might be more willing to compromise and cooperate, seeking win-win solutions in various situations. This transit can be an opportune time to address any lingering conflicts or issues in your relationships with a diplomatic and fair approach.

## 7 Thursday

Change is in the air, with a refreshing breeze of potential arriving to invigorate your social life. This shift connects you with creative individuals who contribute to a more supportive network. Collaborating with a group of kindred spirits allows you to blaze a trail toward new goals and projects. The essence of manifestation raises the bar, tempting you with a wealth of possibilities. Your willingness to embrace new people and opportunities lets you set sail on calmer seas.

**8 Friday**

Moon ingress Aquarius. Mars trine Uranus alignment encourages you to be bold and embrace change as you venture into uncharted territories. Be open to unexpected opportunities that come your way, as they might lead to exciting and fulfilling experiences. Your intuition and ingenuity guide exciting endeavors and breakthroughs. Embrace the spirit of independence and let your creative and forward-thinking nature shine during this empowering cosmic alignment.

**9 Saturday**

With Mars opposing Saturn and Neptune and a Full Moon in the mix, you might face some challenges and conflicting energies. Mars opposed Saturn can create a sense of frustration and limitation, making it difficult to assert yourself or move forward with your plans. The Full Moon can intensify emotions and bring issues to the surface, demanding your attention. You may feel torn between your desires and responsibilities, creating tension.

**10 Sunday**

With the Moon entering Pisces and Mars forming a trine with Pluto, you may experience emotional intensity and empowerment. Your intuition and sensitivity heighten during this time, allowing you to tap into the subtle energies around you. This period encourages you to embrace your inner strength and use it to transform areas of your life that need change and growth. The Mars-Pluto trine brings determination and resilience to face challenges and accomplish your goals.

## 11 Monday

Mercury turns direct. You might find that information flows more smoothly, and you feel more confident in expressing yourself and making essential choices. Take advantage of this momentum to progress in areas that may have felt stagnant or confusing during the retrograde. Remember to stay adaptable and open-minded as you navigate this transition and embrace the newfound clarity and direction that Mercury's direct motion brings.

## 12 Tuesday

With Saturn sextile Uranus, stability and innovation come into harmonious alignment. This aspect encourages you to balance tradition and progressive change, allowing you to build a solid foundation while embracing new, exciting opportunities. Meanwhile, Venus conjunct Jupiter brings joy, abundance, and expansion to relationships and pleasures. This conjunction enhances your social life and brings opportunities for growth in matters of the heart.

## 13 Wednesday

Upcoming options infuse brightness and lightness into your life, setting you on a favorable trend to expand your life. They create synchronistic meetings that foster friendships with unique companions. Your social life deepens and broadens as an emphasis on communication facilitates growing your social life as invitations come rolling in to tempt you out with friends, nurturing your dreams and goals while lighting the path toward developing your skills.

## 14 Thursday

Moon ingress Taurus. Your emotions may become more steady and reliable, allowing you to approach situations calmly and practically. Use this energy to create a strong foundation for your endeavors and nurture your relationships with care and patience. The Moon in Taurus invites you to find contentment in the present moment and embrace the joys of the material world while staying grounded and steady in your emotional responses.

### 15 Friday

With Mercury sextile Mars, you may experience increased mental sharpness and quick thinking. This aspect enhances your ability to express yourself assertively and with confidence. Your communication skills are on point, and you can effectively convey your thoughts to others. It is an excellent time for problem-solving and decision-making, as your mind is agile and focused. You might find yourself motivated to take action and pursue your goals with determination.

### 16 Saturday

With the Moon ingress Gemini, you may feel more curious, adaptable, and socially inclined. This astrological event brings a heightened interest in learning new things and connecting with others. Your mind is agile and open to various ideas and perspectives. It's an excellent time for communication, networking, and intellectual pursuits. You might desire to socialize, exchange ideas, and gather information.

### 17 Sunday

Positive news arrives, spotlighting your potential to explore diverse growth pathways. Taking courageous steps toward learning a new area introduces a time of beginning that expands life. This journey involves social engagement, laughter, and thoughtful discussions stimulated by the exchange of helpful advice that nurtures your energy. Embracing change underscores your willingness to improve your circumstances through the choices and decisions you make for your life.

**18 Monday**

When Mercury forms a sextile with Mars, you may find yourself experiencing increased mental agility and communication skills. Your thoughts and ideas flow easily, and you can assert yourself with confidence and clarity. This harmonious aspect encourages you to act on your plans and maintain your desires. Meanwhile, as the Moon enters Cancer, your emotional landscape may become more sensitive and nurturing.

**19 Tuesday**

You can create plans for future development and tap into your creative talents to yield significant results. Prioritizing your life helps you seize the moment and launch a stunning idea that inspires growth and prosperity. Getting involved in a group project infuses harmonizing energy, promoting well-being. As the heaviness lifts, you spot more opportunities to get involved with kindred spirits and engage with creative collaborators who offer insightful ideas and engaging conversations.

**20 Wednesday**

As the Moon enters Leo, you may notice a surge of self-expression and a desire to shine brightly in your interactions and endeavors today. This celestial event brings a sense of confidence and creativity to your emotional landscape, encouraging you to embrace your unique qualities and share them with the world. You might find yourself seeking attention and recognition, which can be a positive force if channeled into endeavors that align with your passions.

**21 Thursday**

Using innovative solutions and workarounds, you can push obstacles to the side and head towards growth in your life. Your star is ready to shine as you head towards advancement in your working life, with a new day dawning and bringing many opportunities that benefit your circumstances on several levels. You usher in a robust trend into your life, expanding your world. It all adds to a winning chapter of refining your craft and merging dreams with your abilities.

**22 Friday**

Sun ingress Virgo astrological event encourages you to take a more systematic approach to various aspects of your life. You'll likely feel a greater sense of responsibility and a desire to improve your skills and knowledge. This Virgo influence may also prompt you to pay more attention to your health and well-being as you seek to establish better routines and habits. Embrace this time of heightened dedication and productivity as you progress significantly.

**23 Saturday**

With the Moon's ingress into Virgo, combined with the energy of the New Moon, this is a time of fresh beginnings and a heightened focus on practicality and self-improvement for you. Virgo's influence accentuates your attention to detail and encourages you to analyze your goals and aspirations with a critical eye. It's an opportune moment to set new intentions and map out a clear plan. Your emotions are grounded during this lunar phase, allowing for well-informed decisions.

**24 Sunday**

As the Sun forms a square aspect with Uranus, you may experience a sense of restlessness and unpredictability. This planetary alignment can bring sudden changes, surprises, or unexpected events that disrupt your routines and plans. You might seek a break from constraints and embrace your individuality. While this energy can be exhilarating, it's essential to be mindful of impulsive actions and potential clashes with those who might resist your independence.

**25 Monday**

With the Moon's ingress into Libra and Venus' ingress into Leo, you might find a harmonious balance between your emotions and your desires for love and appreciation. Libra's influence fosters a need for peace and harmony in your relationships, encouraging you to seek compromise and cooperation with others. On the other hand, Venus in Leo adds a touch of passion and dramatic flair to your romantic endeavors and social connections.

**26 Tuesday**

The trine to Saturn brings a sense of commitment and reliability to your connections, making it an ideal time to strengthen existing bonds or build new relationships. The sextile to Uranus adds a touch of excitement and spontaneity to your love life, introducing refreshing and unexpected experiences. You may also feel creativity and intuition with the trine to Neptune, making it an excellent time for artistic expression and connecting more spiritually with others.

**27 Wednesday**

Venus opposed Pluto's astrological aspect, which can bring hidden tensions and issues related to trust, control, and intimacy to the surface. You may feel drawn to intense and transformative connections, but avoid getting entangled in unhealthy dynamics or obsessions. This transit is when you might need to confront deep-seated issues within yourself or with others, which can be challenging but liberating in the long run.

**28 Thursday**

As the Moon enters Scorpio, you may notice a heightened intensity in your emotions and a more profound desire for introspection. You will likely experience a more substantial need for privacy and emotional depth during this lunar transit. It is a time when you might find yourself drawn to uncovering hidden truths and exploring the deeper layers of your psyche. Be prepared for heightened intuition and heightened sensitivity to the energies around you.

**29 Friday**

With Uranus forming a sextile aspect to Neptune, you may experience a period of heightened intuition and imaginative inspiration. This astrological alignment encourages you to explore unconventional ideas and embrace your creative and spiritual side. Your instinct may be sharp during this time, allowing you to tap into higher realms of consciousness and gain valuable insights. Allow yourself to dream big and let your imagination guide you on a journey of self-discovery.

**30 Saturday**

Moon ingress Sagittarius. This lunar transit encourages you to embrace a more adventurous and free-spirited approach to life, allowing you to break from routine and venture into uncharted territories. Use this time to broaden your mind, engage in meaningful conversations, and seek wisdom from different sources. Let the Sagittarian energy inspire you to embrace the joy of discovery and embark on a journey of personal growth and understanding.

**31 Sunday**

Developing plans places your goals and dreams at the forefront, igniting progression in your life. Attracting something you've long sought after initiates a new cycle of potential that elevates your aspirations to the next level. It presents a sparkling path that fosters creative inspiration, freedom, and adventure, connecting you with kindred spirits. It encourages you to become actively involved in developing your social life.

# <u>September</u>

| Sun | Mon | Tue | Wed | Thu | Fri | Sat |
|---|---|---|---|---|---|---|
| | 1 | 2 | 3 | 4 | 5 | 6 |
| 7 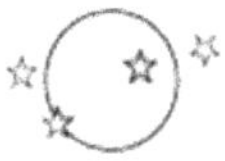 | 8 | 9 | 10 | 11 | 12 | 13 |
| 14  | 15 | 16 | 17 | 18 | 19 | 20 |
| 21  | 22 | 23 | 24 | 25 | 26 | 27 |
| 28 | 29 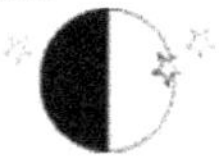 | 30 | | | | |

## NEW MOON

# Corn/Harvest Moon

## SEPTEMBER

**1 Monday**

Saturn's influence in Pisces can bring a sense of spiritual growth and a desire to seek inner wisdom and understanding. It's a time to confront any boundaries or limitations that hinder your emotional growth and to embrace a more intuitive perspective. Be mindful of Saturn in Pisces's lessons, as they can lead to profound spiritual development. Use this period to cultivate a deeper connection to your emotions and to approach challenges with a compassionate and open heart.

**2 Tuesday**

As the Moon enters Capricorn, you may experience a shift towards a more focused and disciplined approach to your emotions. This lunar transit encourages you to prioritize your responsibilities and long-term goals, seeking stability and structure in your emotional life. With Mercury moving into Virgo, your communication style becomes more analytical and precise. You pay attention to the finer details in your interactions and seek practical solutions to any challenges.

**3 Wednesday**

Mercury square Uranus. Embrace the opportunity to break free from mental rigidity and explore fresh approaches to problem-solving. However, be mindful of impulsive communication and hasty decisions. Take a moment to ground yourself and channel the inventive energy of Mercury square Uranus into constructive and creative pursuits that can lead to exciting breakthroughs in your intellectual and communicative endeavors.

**4 Thursday**

As the Moon enters Aquarius, you may experience a shift towards a more open and intellectually curious emotional state. During this lunar transit, you might seek a sense of belonging within a community or a desire to connect with like-minded individuals who share your interests and ideals. Aquarius' influence fosters a heightened sense of independence and a willingness to embrace your unique qualities and perspectives.

**5 Friday**

With Mars forming a square aspect to Jupiter, you may feel a surge of energy and enthusiasm, but exercising caution and avoiding overextending yourself is essential. This astrological influence can lead to a tendency to take on more than you can handle, leading to potential burnout or impulsive actions. While feeling inspired and confident during this transition is natural, be mindful of the need to channel your energies effectively and prioritize your goals.

**6 Saturday**

As the Moon enters Pisces, your emotions may become more empathetic and compassionate, urging you to connect with your intuition and spiritual side. This lunar transit can enhance your sensitivity to the feelings of others and inspire acts of kindness and understanding. Embrace the introspective and empathetic energies of Uranus retrograde and the Moon in Pisces to cultivate a deeper understanding of yourself and others, fostering growth and emotional harmony.

**7 Sunday**

During the Full Moon, you may experience heightened emotions and a sense of culmination. This lunar phase signifies a time of completion and illumination, where things building up come to a head. It's a period of heightened awareness where you can gain insights into your emotions and inner world. You might need balance, harmony in your relationships, and a desire to release any emotional baggage that no longer serves you.

**8 Monday**

As the Moon enters Aries, you may feel a surge of energy and a heightened sense of assertiveness. This lunar transit sparks a desire for action and initiates a dynamic and adventurous period. You might be more impulsive and eager to take on new challenges, making it an excellent time to start fresh projects or enthusiastically pursue your passions. Aries' influence encourages you to embrace your independence and courageously step out of your comfort zone.

**9 Tuesday**

Remaining receptive to change and exploring the array of possibilities in your life propels you beyond a period of stillness and directs you toward growth. Dismantling barriers clears the path for you to chart an exciting journey with profound significance. Trusting your instincts empowers you to pursue your dreams and blaze a trail forward. The unique territory you carve out offers thrilling prospects for your career path.

**10 Wednesday**

Moon ingress Taurus. During this lunar transit, you might feel a more substantial need to indulge in sensory experiences and seek out physical comforts. It's an excellent time to savor delicious meals, spend time in nature, or engage in activities that bring peace and relaxation. The Taurus Moon also encourages you to be patient and steadfast in your endeavors, allowing you to make steady progress toward your goals.

**11 Thursday**

Embracing change and welcoming new possibilities sweeps away stagnant energy, creating space for a lighter atmosphere in your life. A whirlwind of activities on the horizon will bring new dreams and goals into sharp focus. Leveraging your creativity puts the finishing touch on this exciting process, leading you to a valuable opportunity worth pursuing. The launch of an enterprising phase of growth promises that you'll power through to a brighter chapter.

**12 Friday**

With the Sun forming a harmonious sextile to Jupiter, you might experience a period of optimism and expanded opportunities. This astrological alignment encourages you to tap into your confidence and embrace a positive outlook on life. As the Moon moves into Gemini, your emotions may become more adaptable and communicative, encouraging social interactions and intellectual pursuits. This lunar transit opens more curiosity and a desire to explore new perspectives.

**13 Saturday**

Sun conjunct Mercury. During this alignment, your thoughts and ideas align effortlessly with your sense of self, allowing you to express yourself quickly and confidently. Your mind is sharp and receptive, making it a favorable time for learning, problem-solving, and making important decisions. This conjunction enhances your ability to articulate your thoughts, making it easier to convey your message and connect with others effectively.

**14 Sunday**

Nurturing your home life is about to introduce significant changes that shape your path toward growth and progression. This change heralds a new chapter brimming with possibilities that cultivate interpersonal bonds and promote a serene atmosphere filled with thoughtful conversations. It initiates a lively time of open communication, enhancing the foundations of your life. This vibrant phase will be a source of joy and fulfillment for your soul.

**15 Monday**

Moon ingress Cancer is a favorable time to express your emotions openly and supportively to yourself and those you care about. Allow the Cancer Moon to guide you toward a deeper understanding of your emotional landscape, providing a safe space for healing and self-care. Embrace this period to create a harmonious and loving atmosphere, nourishing your soul and fostering meaningful connections with your loved ones.

**16 Tuesday**

Venus sextile Mars astrological alignment brings a delightful blend of passion and diplomacy to your relationships. Your interactions with others are infused with charm and magnetism, making attracting positive attention and creating meaningful connections easier. It is an excellent time for expressing your desires and affections confidently and gently and resolving any conflicts with a sense of understanding and compromise.

**17 Wednesday**

As the Moon enters Leo, you may feel a boost of confidence and a desire for self-expression. This lunar transit encourages you to embrace your inner performer and shine brightly in your interactions. However, with Mercury opposing Saturn, you might encounter communication challenges. You could feel restricted or weighed down by responsibilities and practical concerns. This aspect may create moments of self-doubt or difficulty expressing your thoughts effectively.

**18 Thursday**

As Mercury moves into Libra, you may notice a shift towards more diplomatic and harmonious communication. This astrological transit encourages you to consider different viewpoints and seek compromise in your interactions. You might find yourself more inclined to weigh the pros and cons of various options before making decisions. However, with Mercury opposed to Neptune, there is a potential for confusion and miscommunication.

**19 Friday**

With the Moon's ingress into Virgo and Venus also moving into Virgo, you might focus more on practicality, organization, and attention to detail. This combination of energies encourages you to take a more systematic and analytical approach to your emotions and relationships. It's a favorable time for refining your daily routines, nurturing your well-being, and making meaningful improvements in your connections with others.

**20 Saturday**

Venus Square Uranus' astrological influence can bring unexpected events or encounters that disrupt the status quo. You might crave exciting experiences, seeking new connections and adventures. However, be mindful of the tendency for impulsive decisions or rebellious behavior during this time. The Venus-Uranus square can also create tensions in existing relationships, as a need for freedom and independence clashes with the desire for stability and security.

**21 Sunday**

As the Sun opposes Saturn, you may encounter challenges and obstacles that test your resolve and confidence. This astrological aspect can bring a sense of limitation and responsibility, prompting you to confront areas where you feel restricted or held back. However, with the New Moon and the Moon's ingress into Libra, you are presented with a fresh start and an opportunity to find balance and harmony amidst the challenges.

**22 Monday**

As Mars moves into Scorpio, you may experience a surge of intensity and determination in your actions and desires. This astrological influence can heighten your emotional depth and bring a sense of passion and power to your endeavors. Around the September Equinox, you'll be transitioning into a new season, marking a time of balance and reflection as the day and night are of equal length. As the Sun enters Libra, you'll head towards seeking harmony and fairness.

**23 Tuesday**

When the Sun opposes Neptune, you may experience confusion and a blur between reality and illusion. This astrological aspect can bring a sense of vagueness and uncertainty to your thoughts and actions, making it challenging to see things clearly or make decisive choices. Your emotions might be more susceptible to external influences, leading to feelings of disorientation or vulnerability.

**24 Wednesday**

With the Sun forming trines to Uranus and Pluto, you may experience transformation and empowerment. This astrological alignment enhances your sense of individuality and self-expression. The trine to Uranus encourages you to embrace your uniqueness and seek innovative ways of approaching life. You may feel a surge of creative energy and a desire to break from old patterns. Meanwhile, the trine to Pluto fosters introspection and the potential for inner growth.

**25 Thursday**

Life is becoming busier as change is on the horizon, ushering in news, invitations, and opportunities. Planning and growth will be essential to navigating these options and progressing towards the development of your skills. The upcoming period marks the start of something significant in your life as it shines a light on an area worth your time. Fueling your vision boosts your confidence and enables you to take action, enhancing your energy and propelling your abilities forward.

**26 Friday**

As the Moon moves into Sagittarius, you may feel a sense of adventure and optimism. This lunar transit encourages you to explore new horizons and embrace a more open-minded perspective. Your emotions may be more buoyant and free-spirited as you seek experiences that expand your knowledge and understanding of the world. Sagittarius' influence fosters a love for learning and a desire to seek the truth. It is an excellent time to embark on journeys that enrich your soul.

**27 Saturday**

Fresh options will pave an uncharted path forward, allowing you to dip your toes into a new domain. This transition shines a light on social engagement, collaborations, and ambitious endeavors that nurture creativity. Your openness to exploring new leads brings refreshing options into your life. The arrival of opportunities direct your attention toward self-development and growth. As you work diligently to sharpen your skills, you'll soon uncover intriguing leads.

**28 Sunday**

A window of opportunity is cracking open, setting your life on a course toward greener pastures. Your upcoming journey glows with new possibilities, and staying available to change will facilitate your growth and guide you through unique learning experiences that enrich your life. You're on the cusp of transitioning into a more balanced and stable environment that allows you to develop your dreams with determination.

# October

| Sun | Mon | Tue | Wed | Thu | Fri | Sat |
|---|---|---|---|---|---|---|
| | | | 1 | 2 | 3 | 4 |
| 5 | 6 | 7 | 8 | 9 | 10 | 11 |
| 12 | 13 | 14 | 15 | 16 | 17 | 18 |
| 19 | 20 | 21 | 22 | 23 | 24 | 25 |
| 26 | 27 | 28 | 29 | 30 | 31 | |

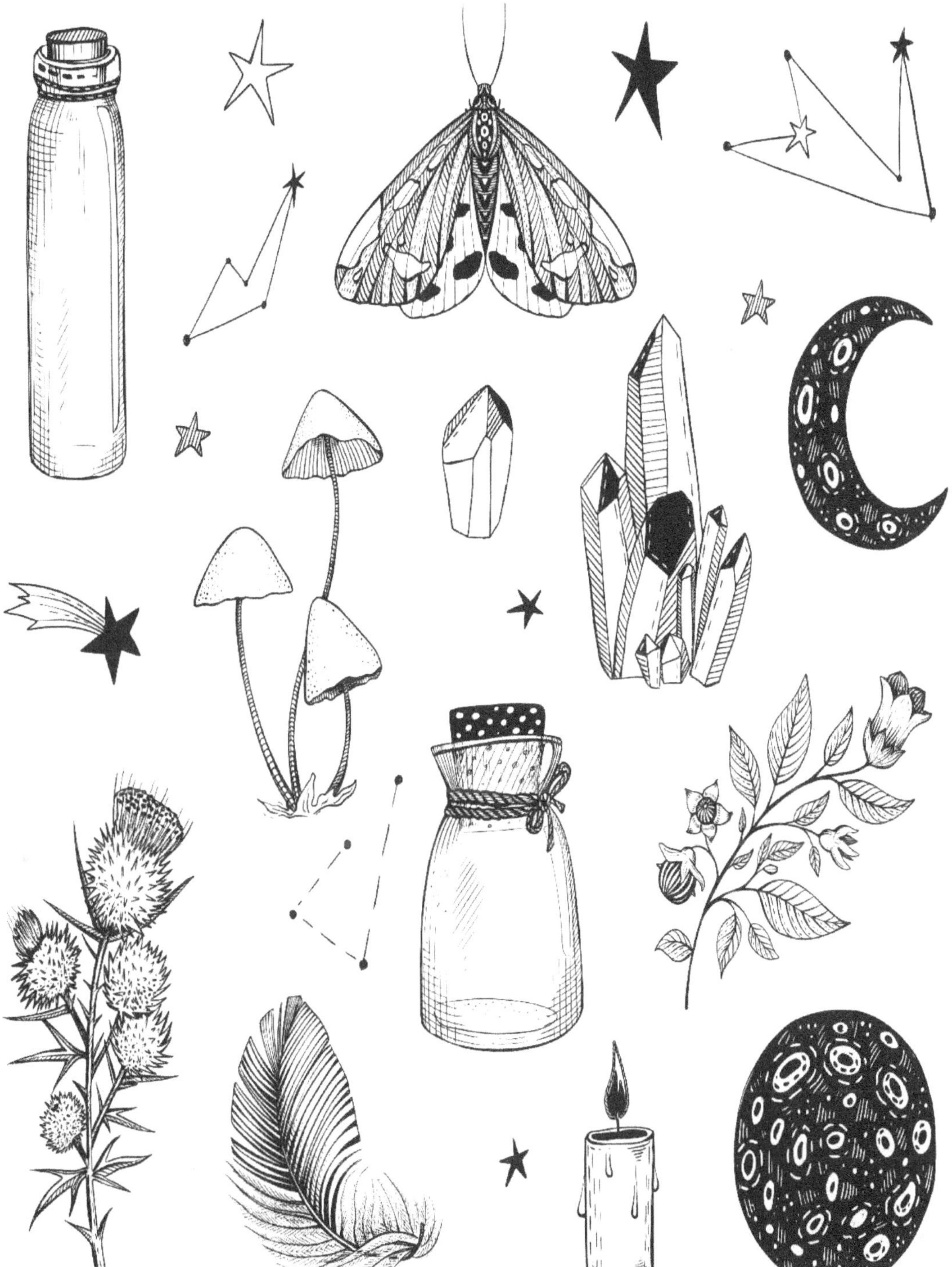

## New Moon

## HUNTERS MOON

**29 Monday**

Moon ingress Capricorn lunar transit may prompt you to assess your commitments and consider the areas of your life that require more stability and organization. Embrace the grounded and steady energy of the Capricorn Moon to take charge of your emotions and pursue your ambitions with perseverance and purpose. Allow this period to empower you to build a solid foundation for future success and personal growth.

**30 Tuesday**

This period ushers in a busy time, sparking adaptability and new adventures. Inspiration soars, creating a peak for your creativity and drawing a wealth of unique growth pathways. You stumble upon an assignment that highlights your talents and allows your gifts to shine. It encourages you to delve into projects that facilitate growth. Collaboration within a group environment with other trailblazers forms a strong foundation for joint endeavors and collaborations.

**1 Wednesday**

As the Moon enters Aquarius, you may experience a heightened curiosity and a desire for intellectual exploration. This astrological influence encourages you to think outside the box and embrace unconventional ideas. However, with Mercury square Jupiter, there's a potential for information overload or exaggeration. This aspect can lead to overconfidence in your opinions or a tendency to overlook important details.

**2 Thursday**

Opportunities on the horizon bring a positive aspect that allows you to start fresh. These opportunities inspire creativity and keep you at the top of your game, expanding your life into new areas. They provide ample time for you to invest your energy into developing the right path forward for your life while also nurturing your growing abilities. As you share your work with others, you embark on an expressive journey that connects identity and creativity.

## OCTOBER

**3 Friday**

Change is in the air as you explore a community setting with friends and companions, nurturing well-being and harmony. It opens the door to a fresh start that leads to a more connected environment. Thoughtful discussions and insightful conversations stir the pot of manifestation in your world, generating ideas and options that expand your horizons. Good fortune flows in, finding its place among happiness and harmony, offering you improved circumstances.

**4 Saturday**

Moon ingress Pisces astrological influence encourages you to connect with your intuition and tap into the deeper currents of your emotions. The Pisces energy fosters a dreamy and imaginative atmosphere, making it an ideal time for creative activities and introspection. You might find yourself more attuned to the needs and feelings of others, fostering a greater sense of compassion and understanding. Permit yourself to find solace in this lunar phase's quiet moments.

**5 Sunday**

As notable changes approach, they highlight a journey that nurtures your life. This healing influence removes outworn areas, enabling you to embark on an approach that promotes growth and rising prospects. Your confidence, drive, and creativity increase to meet the challenges of expanding your life outwardly. Keeping your eyes open for fresh possibilities allows you to move forward with a sense of purpose, fostering lively discussions in a stable and happy environment.

**6 Monday**

Moon ingress Aries astrological influence encourages you to take the initiative and enthusiastically pursue your goals. Aries' energy fosters a pioneering spirit, making it an excellent time to start new projects or tackle challenges head-on. However, as Mercury enters Scorpio, your thinking becomes more intense and focused. This transit encourages you to delve deep into matters, seeking hidden truths and uncovering underlying motivations.

**7 Tuesday**

It's essential to be cautious of manipulation and confrontations during this time. The Full Moon and Mercury square Pluto combine to invite you to navigate through intense emotions and interactions, fostering a balance between expressing your feelings and maintaining respectful communication. Embrace the opportunity for growth and transformation by addressing any issues with honesty and a willingness to find common ground.

**8 Wednesday**

You may experience more emotional stability and comfort as the Moon moves into Taurus. This astrological influence encourages you to find pleasure in simple and sensory experiences. At the same time, with Venus forming a sextile to Jupiter, you may feel a heightened sense of joy and optimism in your relationships and pursuits. This alignment fosters a positive and harmonious atmosphere, encouraging you to connect with others warmly and affectionately.

**9 Thursday**

Exploring options helps you unearth new leads for your working life, providing a breakthrough regarding your career path. Planning your journey ignites a new perspective on your situation, spurring the opening of a new chapter driven by the progression that shines radiantly on the horizon. Your commitment and focus enable you to achieve the correct result, building stable foundations and advancing your life by embracing change.

**10 Friday**

As the Moon enters Gemini, you may notice a shift towards increased curiosity and mental activity. This astrological influence encourages you to engage in diverse conversations and explore various topics of interest. Gemini's energy fosters a love for learning and communication, making it an excellent time to connect with others through meaningful discussions. Your emotions become more adaptable and open-minded, allowing you to see different perspectives.

**11 Saturday**

Venus, as opposed to Saturn's astrological aspect, can bring a sense of distance to matters of the heart and may bring feelings of loneliness or a heightened awareness of the responsibilities and commitments that come with your connections. It's essential to be aware of tendencies to self-criticism or pessimism during this time, as the Venus-Saturn opposition can sometimes lead to a lack of self-worth or doubts about your ability to receive love and appreciation.

**12 Sunday**

As the Moon moves into Cancer, you may notice a shift towards a more nurturing and emotional state. This astrological influence encourages you to connect with your feelings profoundly and seek comfort and security in your surroundings. Cancer's energy fosters a sense of empathy and a desire to care for yourself and those around you. During this lunar transit, you might find solace in spending time at home or with loved ones and engaging in activities that evoke nostalgia.

**13 Monday**

Libra's energy fosters a desire for fairness and cooperation, making it an ideal time to focus on partnerships and social interactions. During this Venus transit, you might find yourself more attuned to aesthetics and drawn to art, culture, and anything that brings aesthetic pleasure. Your sense of diplomacy and ability to compromise may also heighten, allowing you to navigate relationships with grace and understanding.

**14 Tuesday**

Venus opposed Neptune's astrological aspect, which can bring a sense of enchantment and a potential for confusion in matters of the heart. Be cautious of projecting unrealistic expectations onto others. With Pluto turning direct, transformative energy encourages you to confront deeper truths and embrace personal growth. As the Moon moves into Leo, your emotions become more vibrant and expressive.

**15 Wednesday**

You touch down on a landscape filled with new potential, offering room to develop your abilities as you take on unique assignments that showcase talents and illuminate pathways for sharing your skills with a broader audience. A positive influence transitions you toward learning new areas as you find your groove, expand life outwardly, and thrive in a more vibrant landscape, with the conditions for growth ripening and allowing you to achieve more progression.

**16 Thursday**

As the Moon moves into Virgo, you may notice a shift towards a more practical and detail-oriented approach to your emotions. This astrological transition encourages you to focus on organization, efficiency, and taking care of practical matters. Virgo's energy fosters a desire for order and a willingness to improve your daily routines. During this lunar transit, you might find solace in tending to tasks that require attention to detail and precision.

**17 Friday**

Sun square Jupiter's astrological influence can bring a sense of enthusiasm and a desire to take on new challenges. However, avoiding overestimating your capabilities or becoming overly confident is essential. There's a potential for taking on too much or being unrealistic in your expectations. While this square can enhance your aspirations and encourage you to dream big, balancing your ambitious energy with a practical approach is crucial.

**18 Saturday**

You may find yourself at a crossroads, with a choice to make that could have a sink-or-swim feeling. Your priorities are currently shifting, and this change prompts you to transform as you move toward a busy period that will help you resolve sensitive areas. By adopting an abundant mindset, you expand the playing field, fostering positivity and marking a significant turning point as a social environment draws kinship and companionship into your life.

**19 Sunday**

Moon ingress Libra astrological transition encourages you to seek fairness and cooperation in your relationships. Libra's energy fosters a desire to connect with others on a deeper level and to create an atmosphere of mutual understanding. During this lunar transition, you might find yourself more attuned to the needs and perspectives of those around you, making it an excellent time for open conversations and finding common ground.

## OCTOBER

**20 Monday**

When Mercury is conjunct with Mars, you may experience heightened mental energy and assertiveness. This astrological alignment can bring a dynamic combination of quick thinking and decisive action. Your thoughts and communication become more direct and assertive, allowing you to express yourself clearly and confidently. This conjunction enhances your problem-solving abilities, making it excellent for logical reasoning and strategic thinking.

**21 Tuesday**

With the arrival of the New Moon, you have fresh opportunities on the horizon. This astrological phase marks a time of setting intentions and planting seeds for the future. As the Moon moves into Scorpio, your emotions may become more intense and introspective. This lunar transition encourages you to delve deeper into your feelings and explore hidden aspects of yourself. Scorpio's energy fosters a desire for transformation and a willingness to confront emotional challenges.

**22 Wednesday**

With Neptune moving into Pisces, you may experience a profound shift in your intuitive and spiritual awareness. This astrological transition fosters a deep connection to your inner world and the subtle energies around you. Neptune's energy encourages you to tap into your imagination and embrace a more compassionate and empathetic outlook. During this period, you might seek artistic and creative pursuits that allow you to connect with the divine.

**23 Thursday**

Sun ingress Scorpio's astrological transition encourages you to explore the depths of your emotions and motivations. Scorpio's energy fosters a sense of intensity and a willingness to face the shadows within yourself and others. It is a time for transformation and regeneration as you seek to release what no longer serves you and embrace personal growth. The Sun's journey through Scorpio invites you to shed what no longer serves you and emerge renewed.

**24 Friday**

As the Moon moves into Sagittarius, you may experience a sense of adventurous and expansive energy. This astrological influence encourages you to seek new experiences and broaden your horizons. However, the Sun square Pluto has the potential for inner and outer power struggles. This aspect may prompt you to confront hidden truths and make transformative changes. On a brighter note, the Mercury trine Jupiter brings an optimistic mental outlook.

**25 Saturday**

When Mercury forms a trine aspect to Saturn, you may experience a period of enhanced focus and mental discipline. This astrological alignment empowers you to approach tasks and communication practically and precisely. Your thoughts become more organized, and your ability to plan and strategize heightens. This trine encourages you to take a patient and methodical approach to your endeavors, allowing you to make steady progress toward your goals.

**26 Sunday**

As the Moon moves into Capricorn, you may notice a shift towards a more goal-oriented emotional state. This astrological transition encourages you to focus on your responsibilities and work towards your ambitions. Capricorn's energy fosters a sense of determination and a willingness to put in the effort to achieve your desired outcomes. During this lunar transition, you might find satisfaction in making practical progress and taking steps toward your long-term goals.

**27 Monday**

Numerous work-related options provide a chance to explore expansion, searching for leads to nurture results. Unexpected inspiration gives you a boost of creativity, redoubling your efforts to prepare and launch a project in your life. At the same time, a new perspective fuels your energy and enthusiasm for new endeavors. With rising imagination at your disposal, the projects initiated have the potential to reach fruition.

**28 Tuesday**

With Mars forming a trine to Jupiter, you may experience increased energy and a sense of optimism. This astrological alignment empowers you with the courage to take on challenges and pursue your goals with enthusiasm. Your actions become more expansive and driven, and you may find it easier to overcome obstacles and achieve success. This trine encourages you to step out of your comfort zone and explore new horizons, enhancing self-confidence and assertiveness.

**29 Wednesday**

As the Moon moves into Aquarius, you may experience a shift towards a more open and progressive emotional outlook. This astrological transition encourages you to embrace individuality and seek unique experiences. With Mercury forming a trine with Neptune, your communication has an added touch of imagination and sensitivity. This aspect fosters creative and intuitive thinking, making it a favorable time for artistic pursuits and heartfelt conversations.

**30 Thursday**

With Mercury forming a sextile to Pluto, you may experience a period of deep insights and profound understanding. This astrological alignment empowers you to uncover hidden truths beneath the surface. Your communication becomes more perceptive, and your thinking more analytical, allowing you to grasp complex concepts quickly. This sextile encourages you to engage in meaningful conversations that have the potential to transform your perspectives.

## NOVEMBER

| Sun | Mon | Tue | Wed | Thu | Fri | Sat |
|---|---|---|---|---|---|---|
| | | | | | | 1 |
| 2 | 3 | 4 | 5 | 6 | 7 | 8 |
| 9 | 10 | 11 | 12 | 13 | 14 | 15 |
| 16 | 17 | 18 | 19 | 20 | 21 | 22 |
| 23 | 24 | 25 | 26 | 27 | 28 | 29 |
| 30 | | | | | | |

## New Moon

# <u>Beaver Moon</u>

**31 Friday**

As the Moon moves into Pisces, you may notice a shift towards heightened sensitivity and emotional depth. This astrological transition encourages you to tap into your intuition and connect with your inner world. Pisces' energy fosters a sense of compassion and empathy, making it a favorable time to communicate with others more profoundly and offer support where needed. During this lunar transit, you might find solace in creative activities or moments of introspection.

**1 Saturday**

Change is in the air, signaling a time of sharing with friends and companions. Thoughtful discussions bring forth ideas and options that ignite your interest. Engaging with your broader circle of friends provides a secure foundation for you to inspire your creative abilities. The purposeful push toward your goals generates momentum that charts a course toward a rising aspect in your life, ushering in an era of lightness and expansion.

**2 Sunday**

Moon ingress Aries With the Moon moving into Aries, and you may experience a surge of assertive energy and a desire to take action. This astrological shift encourages you to embrace a more self-driven and proactive approach to your emotions. Aries' energy fosters independence and a determination to pursue your desires. However, with Venus square Jupiter, there's potential for overindulgence or unrealistic expectations in matters of the heart.

## NOVEMBER

**3 Monday**

Charting a course towards a brighter chapter and entering a growth-orientated time brings a productive landscape into view. As you head into this opportunity-laden period, it takes you towards unique areas that grow your talents. Doing research and proactively developing the path lets you immerse yourself in merging your abilities with an approach that captures inspiration and refining skills. It gives you the green light to grow your career, attracting advancement.

**4 Tuesday**

Mars trine Neptune astrological alignment empowers you to channel your energy into imaginative pursuits and connect with your intuitive side. As Mars moves into Sagittarius, your actions become fueled by a desire for exploration and growth. This energy encourages you to step out of your comfort zone and embrace new experiences. However, with the Moon moving into Taurus, there's a shift towards a more grounded and practical emotional state.

**5 Wednesday**

During a Full Moon, you may experience a heightened sense of culmination and illumination. This astrological phase marks a time of bringing matters to fruition and gaining clarity on situations that have been developing. The Full Moon's energy encourages you to reflect on your goals, intentions, and progress, allowing you to assess what needs completion and adjustments. It is a time when you might find your feelings more pronounced and your intuition more substantial.

**6 Thursday**

Mars sextile Pluto astrological alignment empowers you to take action on your goals with strategic focus. As the Moon moves into Gemini, your emotions become more adaptable and communicative, encouraging you to engage in lively conversations and gather information. Meanwhile, with Venus moving into Scorpio, your emotional connections and desires may deepen as Scorpio's energy fosters a passion for profound and transformative relationship experiences.

**7 Friday**

Potential lies on the periphery of your life, and a more stable landscape allows you to channel your energy productively into a meaningful journey forward. The arrival of new options supports growth in your social life, and lighter energy triggers cascading possibilities that nurture your life. This period also introduces a networking aspect, providing companionship with friends. As you work to improve circumstances, you foster lively discussions in a happy environment.

**8 Saturday**

As Uranus moves into Taurus, you may enter a period of change and innovation in areas related to your values and resources. This astrological transition encourages you to embrace new ways of approaching stability and material matters. However, Venus Square Pluto has the potential for intense emotional dynamics in relationships and financial issues. This aspect can lead to power struggles or transformations in your connections.

**9 Sunday**

When Mercury turns retrograde, you may experience a period of introspection and reevaluation. This astrological phase often brings challenges and miscommunications in communication, travel, and technology. It's a time to exercise caution in signing contracts or making significant decisions, as information might be unclear or hidden. This period invites you to reflect on past choices and revisit unfinished projects.

**10 Monday**

Moon ingress Leo astrological transition encourages you to embrace your creativity and seek out opportunities for self-expression. Leo's energy fosters a desire for recognition and a willingness to shine in the spotlight. During this lunar transit, you might crave activities that showcase your talents and engage in enjoyable and playful experiences. The Leo Moon encourages you to tap into your inner confidence and embrace a sense of joy and spontaneity.

**11 Tuesday**

As Jupiter turns retrograde, you may experience a period of introspection and inner growth. This astrological shift encourages you to look within and reassess your beliefs, values, and aspirations. While Jupiter retrograde can sometimes bring a slowdown in external expansion, it offers an opportunity to refine your goals and seek wisdom from your past experiences. This period prompts you to explore your philosophy and consider how it aligns with your life's direction.

**12 Wednesday**

With Mercury forming a conjunction with Mars, you may experience a period of heightened mental agility and assertiveness. This astrological alignment empowers you to think quickly and communicate directly and confidently. Your mind becomes more focused and decisive, making it a favorable time for making decisions and acting on your ideas. As the Moon moves into Virgo, your emotions may become more attuned to practicality and organization.

**13 Thursday**

A transformational cycle commences in your life, dispelling doubt and bringing forth the preparation of plans. It provides a firm direction as you prioritize the development of cutting-edge ideas and opportunities, flourishing in creativity, and embracing an abundance of happiness and purpose. An important project you work on becomes a hub of activity, drawing purposefulness and joy into your life, opening a journey that is both enriching and joyful.

**14 Friday**

The options that lie ahead illuminate an exciting path for your life, one characterized by meaningful connections, social engagement, and insightful discussions. As you engage with your broader circle of friends, you find replenishment for your emotional well-being. This path crafts a journey rich in meaningful moments shared with friends, and a positive trend sees life gaining momentum as invitations open doors to rising prospects.

**15 Saturday**

As the Moon moves into Libra, you may notice a shift towards a greater emphasis on balance and harmony in your emotions and interactions. This astrological transition encourages you to seek fairness and cooperation in your relationships. Libra's energy fosters a desire for companionship and a willingness to find common ground. During this lunar transition, you might seek social activities and engage in conversations that create understanding and unity.

**16 Sunday**

Your world is brimming with possibility and potential as you discover new sources of prosperity. These sources attract people who radiate positive energy into your life. You soon receive bright and joyful news that fills you with optimism about expanding the horizons of your life. This newfound confidence prepares you to engage with the broader world of social opportunities. The invitations you receive encourage thoughtful discussions and foster connections that enhance your world.

**17 Monday**

With the Sun forming trines to Jupiter and Saturn, you may experience a balanced period. This astrological alignment empowers you with optimism and discipline, allowing you to blend expansion with practicality. As Mercury sextiles Pluto, your thoughts become more profound and insightful. Additionally, with the Moon moving into Scorpio, your emotions may become more intense and introspective. This cosmic combination encourages you to harness your inner strength.

**18 Tuesday**

New opportunities ahead pave the way for a productive path. Developing your ideas introduces purposefulness and encourages teamwork. It enables you to veer away from doubt and anxiety, moving forward with courage and conviction towards your dreams. Extending your reach into a unique area empowers you to dabble with your abilities and nurture your talents while rising prospects bring a refreshing tailwind of growth and prosperity.

**19 Wednesday**

Mercury ingress Scorpio astrological transition encourages you to explore the hidden corners of your thoughts and engage in conversations with a heightened level of perception. However, with Mercury opposing Uranus, your communication has the potential for unconventional ideas. This aspect might challenge you to embrace new perspectives and adapt to changes in your thought patterns. The Mercury trine Neptune aspect adds intuition and creativity.

**20 Thursday**

Embrace the New Moon's energy to initiate new projects or habits that resonate with your authentic self. As Mercury enters Sagittarius, embrace the spirit of adventure in your communication and exploration of new horizons. The Uranus-Neptune sextile invites you to channel your innovative ideas into tangible expressions that can contribute to your personal and creative growth during this dynamic and promising period.

**21 Friday**

Sun-opposed Uranus astrological aspect can bring restless energy, prompting you to seek excitement and innovation. However, with the Sun trine Neptune, a harmonious influence encourages you to blend your individuality with a sense of compassion and empathy. This aspect inspires you to tap into your creative and spiritual depths, fostering a deeper connection to your inner self and the world around you.

**22 Saturday**

As Mercury forms a trine to Saturn, you convey your thoughts with clarity and precision. With the Moon moving into Capricorn, your emotions may lean towards practicality and a focus on goals. The Mercury trine Jupiter aspect positively influences your thinking, supporting you in pursuing new opportunities and broadening your intellectual horizons. Embrace the Sagittarius Sun's energy to fuel your curiosity and seek experiences that align with your beliefs.

**23 Sunday**

With the Sun forming a sextile to Pluto, you may experience a period of empowerment and transformation. This astrological alignment empowers you to tap into your inner strength and make positive changes in your life. The Sun's energy intensifies, encouraging you to embrace the potential for growth and renewal. This aspect invites you to engage in activities that promote personal empowerment and shed light on any hidden parts of yourself.

**24 Monday**

A windfall comes knocking and gives you an exciting sign that things are ready to shift forward in your career path, with noticeable changes ahead drawing growth and progression, letting you blaze a trail toward expansion. Rising prospects help you gain traction in developing your goals, bringing impressive results that improve your life. News arrives, sparking excitement as tangible results bring the correct result into your life, enabling you to feel proud of what you are achieving.

**25 Tuesday**

With Mercury forming a conjunction with Venus, you may experience a period of enhanced communication and social harmony. This astrological alignment empowers you with a balanced blend of thoughtfulness and charm in your interactions. Your conversations may become more pleasant and agreeable, fostering connections with others. As the Moon moves into Aquarius, your emotions may become more detached and focused on intellectual pursuits.

**26 Wednesday**

Venus trines Jupiter. Venus trine Saturn. This combination invites you to find a sweet spot between the joy of exploring new horizons and the wisdom of maintaining commitment and responsibility. Embrace these Venus trines' energy to cultivating positive interactions, seek personal growth, and build fulfilling and enduring relationships as you navigate this period of alignment and balance in matters of the heart and personal values.

**27 Thursday**

As the Moon moves into Pisces on Thanksgiving, you may feel the emotional depth and empathy pervading the festivities. This astrological transition encourages you to embrace a spirit of compassion and connection with your loved ones. Pisces' energy fosters a sense of unity and a desire to create a warm and nurturing atmosphere. It's a time when you may feel more attuned to the emotional needs of those around you.

**28 Friday**

Saturn turns direct astrological event signals a time to apply the lessons and wisdom gained during its retrograde phase. You might find it easier to tackle long-term goals and commitments with renewed determination. Saturn's direct motion encourages you to take stock of your ambitions and work diligently towards them, now with a clearer understanding of the challenges and responsibilities ahead. Let Saturn's retrograde guide you toward personal growth and achievement.

**29 Saturday**

As Mercury turns direct, you may sense a welcome shift in your daily life. This astrological event marks the end of a period of potential communication challenges, delays, and miscommunications that can occur during Mercury's retrograde phase. With Mercury moving forward, you'll likely notice greater clarity in your thoughts, more fluid communication, and a smoother flow in your everyday activities.

**30 Sunday**

Moon ingress Aries astrological transition can inspire you to take action, assert your needs, and pursue your desires with newfound vigor. However, as Venus opposes Uranus, expect potential disruptions or surprises in the heart and finances. This aspect could bring about unexpected changes in your relationships or values. On a positive note, the Venus trine Neptune aspect adds romantic and dreamy energy to your connections, fostering compassion and creativity.

# December

| Sun | Mon | Tue | Wed | Thu | Fri | Sat |
| --- | --- | --- | --- | --- | --- | --- |
| | 1 | 2 | 3 | 4 | 5 | 6 |
| 7 | 8 | 9 | 10 | 11 | 12 | 13 |
| 14 | 15 | 16 | 17 | 18 | 19 | 20 |
| 21 | 22 | 23 | 24 | 25 | 26 | 27 |
| 28 | 29 | 30 | 31 | | | |

# New Moon

# COLD MOON

## DECEMBER

**1 Monday**

You are on the brink of entering a cycle of expanded possibilities. Your ability to make the best choices for your current situation guides you toward greater happiness in your world. The rising confidence within you propels you forward, motivating you to explore potential avenues for growth. It encourages you to investigate promising leads and ideas that hold significant promise for your life. Life fills with opportunities to socialize, fostering progress and connection.

**2 Tuesday**

Moon ingress Taurus astrological transition encourages you to seek comfort and stability in your surroundings and relationships. Taurus' energy fosters a desire for security and enjoying life's simple pleasures. As Venus forms a sextile to Pluto, your interactions and desires may take on a more intense and transformative quality. This aspect can deepen your connections and add a touch of passion to your encounters.

**3 Wednesday**

You uncover an exciting opportunity that broadens your horizons. Nurturing your talents draws a greater degree of happiness and success into your life. Engagement in a unique and lively domain builds secure foundations, fostering a vibrant environment for cultivating your abilities. Embracing adaptability, adventure, and creativity propels you forward on a purposeful journey to achieve your goals, yielding a pleasing result.

**4 Thursday**

With the Moon moving into Gemini and heralding a Full Moon, you may feel heightened communication and mental activity. This astrological phase typically marks a time of culmination and clarity. Emotions and intentions building since the New Moon may come to fruition and bring insights. Gemini's energy encourages intellectual curiosity and a desire to engage in conversations and share ideas.

**5 Friday**

You're on the brink of discovering a unique realm of potential that beckons to you. This uncharted territory connects your life with an area rich in growth prospects. A sense of celebration and excitement accompanies a significant revelation, allowing you to connect with inspiration. Your social life is poised to yield rising prospects that nurture a landscape brimming with potential. Overcoming perceived limitations unveils a unique opportunity for your life.

**6 Saturday**

With the Moon moving into Cancer, you may experience a desire for nurturing and security. Embrace the Cancer Moon's energy to create a cozy and supportive environment while allowing the Mercury-Neptune trine to inspire you to communicate with depth and emotional understanding. Use this cosmic synergy to foster a sense of security and connection as you navigate this heightened emotional awareness and heartfelt expression.

**7 Sunday**

Exciting changes lie ahead, heralding a change of pace and an invitation to mingle. These developments bring an uptick of potential for your social life. Exciting news provides you with the chance to step up and share with friends. A lighter approach draws sunny skies overhead and leads you to share outings with valued companions. You blaze a trail toward a happy and supportive journey, with thoughtful communication offering an abundance of happiness.

**8 Monday**

News is on the horizon, bringing an expansion. It introduces a group environment and provides an opportunity to work with your creative talents. A river of unique possibilities emerges within your broader social network, serving as the gateway to growing your life. Your social schedule fills up with opportunities to mingle, paving the way for progress and possibility and generating a lively environment filled with opportunities to connect with friends.

**9 Tuesday**

As Mars forms a square to Saturn, you may encounter frustration and limitations in your actions and endeavors. This astrological aspect can bring about obstacles, delays, or a feeling of being held back in your pursuits. It's a time when your energy and ambitions may clash with the need for caution and patience. While this can be a challenging phase, it also offers an opportunity to reassess your goals and refine your strategies.

**10 Wednesday**

With Mercury opposed to Uranus, expect potential communication and thought pattern disruptions. Embrace the Virgo Moon's energy to attend to practical matters and strive for precision while using Neptune's direct motion to trust your instincts and tap into your inner wisdom. Navigate the Mercury-Uranus opposition with adaptability and an open mind, allowing it to inspire innovative solutions and new perspectives as you move through this dynamic period.

**11 Thursday**

With Mercury forming a trine to Neptune, you may experience a period of heightened intuition and creative inspiration. This astrological alignment empowers your communication and thinking with a touch of dreaminess and empathy. It's a favorable time for expressing your ideas and emotions with sensitivity and compassion. As Mercury moves into Sagittarius, your thoughts and conversations may be more adventurous and open-minded.

**12 Friday**

As the Moon moves into Libra, you may notice a shift towards a more harmonious and balanced emotional state. This astrological transition encourages you to seek fairness and cooperation in your interactions with others. Libra's energy fosters a desire for companionship and a willingness to find common ground. During this lunar transit, you might find yourself drawn to social activities and engaging in conversations that create understanding and unity.

**13 Saturday**

With Mercury forming a sextile to Pluto, you might experience a period of intensified mental clarity and insight. This astrological alignment empowers your thoughts and communication with a profound and transformative quality. You may find it easier to delve into deep and meaningful conversations or research topics that require in-depth exploration. This aspect can also enhance your ability to uncover hidden truths and tap into your inner wisdom.

**14 Sunday**

When Mars forms a square to Neptune, you may grapple with confusion and a lack of clear direction in your actions and desires. This astrological aspect can create a sense of inner conflict and make it challenging to assert yourself effectively. It's as though your motivations and intentions are clouded by uncertainty, making it essential to exercise caution in your decision-making and avoid impulsive actions.

**15 Monday**

Moon ingress Scorpio. Mars ingress Capricorn. This combination lets you channel your emotional intensity into productive and purposeful endeavors. Use the Scorpio Moon's energy to embrace self-reflection and emotional healing while allowing Mars in Capricorn to influence you to take systematic steps toward your goals. It's a time to harness your inner strength and resilience as you navigate this period with a focus on personal growth and achievement.

**16 Tuesday**

Change is in the air, signaling a time of sharing with friends and companions. Thoughtful discussions bring forth ideas and options that ignite your interest. Engaging with your broader circle of friends provides a secure foundation for you to inspire your creative abilities. The purposeful push toward your goals generates momentum that charts a course toward a rising aspect in your life, ushering in an era of lightness and expansion.

**17 Wednesday**

With the Sun forming a square to Saturn, you might sense a temporary clash between your desire for self-expression and the constraints of responsibility. It can bring obstacles that may test your patience. It's as though there's a tension between your ambitions and the limitations you face, which can feel frustrating. However, as the Moon moves into Sagittarius, you're encouraged to seek a broader perspective. Sagittarius' energy fosters optimism and a thirst for adventure.

**18 Thursday**

Unexpected developments bring a happy surprise into your life, orienting you towards growing your social life and getting a time of engagement and fun into your world. Friends, fun, and companionship energize your social life, and this trend continues as you infuse bonds with an optimistic and upbeat approach. Confidence rises, and your ability to attract people into your circle becomes magnetic, bringing an influx of messages and communication.

**19 Friday**

Settling into a new groove is facilitated by the changes ahead, bringing happy surprises that connect with your social life. Directing your attention towards sharing and spending time in a supportive and nurturing environment is your focus. A positive influence ahead lets you touch down in a vibrant landscape of possibility, bringing harmony into your life as you get involved in sharing engaging conversations and thoughtful dialogues with kindred spirits.

**20 Saturday**

The Black Moon's ingress into Sagittarius brings a sense of mystery and depth to your quest for knowledge and adventure. This cosmic alignment invites you to explore your psyche's uncharted territories and enthusiastically embrace the unknown. Use the energy of the New Moon to initiate your intentions, drawing upon the Capricorn Moon's dedication and the Sagittarius Black Moon's thirst for wisdom and expansion.

**21 Sunday**

The December Solstice marks the official start of winter in the Northern Hemisphere, emphasizing the need for inner reflection and finding light amidst darkness. As the Sun moves into Capricorn, you're encouraged to embrace a disciplined approach to your responsibilities. Use this cosmic interplay as an opportunity to navigate the complexities of life with wisdom and resilience as you move through this period of introspection and transition into a new season.

**22 Monday**

As the Moon moves into Aquarius, you may sense a shift towards a more open-minded and intellectually oriented emotional state. This astrological transition encourages you to embrace individuality and express your feelings uniquely and unconventionally. Aquarius' energy fosters a desire for freedom, innovation, and community. You might be drawn to social gatherings or activities with individuals who share your interests and ideals.

**23 Tuesday**

Opportunities to socialize bring a connected vibe, with the winds of change carrying news, offering rising prospects. It improves the foundations by bringing more balance, giving you the green light to move forward and become involved with sharing with friends and companions. A carefree chapter springs to life, putting a boost in your step as unique possibilities tempt you out and about, with a situation you channel energy into blossoming into a meaningful path forward.

**24 Wednesday**

With Venus forming a square to Neptune, you may feel a sense of ambiguity and potential challenges in the heart and finances. This astrological aspect can bring about confusion and make it difficult to see things clearly in your relationships and resources. It's essential to avoid making impulsive decisions, especially regarding investments or matters of love. Simultaneously, a more grounded and practical energy prevails as Venus moves into Capricorn.

**25 Thursday**

On Christmas Day, as the Moon gracefully moves into Pisces, you may experience a sense of enchantment and emotional depth. This astrological transition sets the stage for a day of heightened sensitivity and compassion. Pisces' energy fosters a desire for connection with your innermost emotions and a profound empathy for others. It's a perfect time to embrace the spirit of giving, kindness, and understanding that the holiday season represents.

**26 Friday**

Manifestation fuels the crafting of plans for future growth. A social aspect adds glamour and possibility to your life. News arrives, releasing the heaviness and transforming your vision, sweeping away outworn energy to create space for inspiration to light the path forward. New energy brews in the background of your life, attracting a golden phase of growth and prosperity, ruling a happy chapter that fosters social connection and harmony.

**27 Saturday**

With the Moon shifting into Aries, you might feel a surge of dynamic energy and a strong desire to take initiative. This astrological transition encourages you to embrace a bold, assertive approach to your emotions and actions. Aries' energy fosters a sense of independence and a willingness to confront challenges head-on. During this time, you may be more inclined to assert your needs and tackle tasks with determination and enthusiasm.

**28 Sunday**

Noticeable changes ahead attract happiness and abundance into your life, aligning you for growing your circle of friends. Emphasizing expansion brings a breakthrough that offers productive times shared with like-minded people you value. Constructive dialogues provide a thoughtful perspective, bringing new ideas and concepts to explore. It also sparks a creative viewpoint, with a sense of adventure helping you initiate a way forward toward unique endeavors.

**29 Monday**

Moon ingress Taurus. During this time, you might find solace in indulging your senses, whether through enjoying a delicious meal, appreciating art and beauty, or spending time in nature. This lunar influence also supports practicality and a steady approach to your emotions. Use this cosmic alignment to create a sense of tranquility and to nurture your well-being, allowing your emotional landscape to flourish in the serene and sensory-rich environment that Taurus encourages.

**30 Tuesday**

When Mercury forms a square aspect with Saturn, you may encounter challenges in communicating and thinking. This aspect can bring about a sense of restriction and hesitation in your speech and thought processes. You might find it difficult to express yourself clearly, often feeling the weight of self-doubt or fear of judgment when sharing your ideas. It's as if you grapple with limitations and obstacles that can make effective communication and decision-making more strenuous.

**31 Wednesday**

As the Moon enters Gemini on New Year's Eve, you might feel curious and social energy. This astrological shift could inspire you to seek lively and engaging conversations, as Gemini is associated with communication and intellectual stimulation. You may feel drawn to festivities involving mingling with friends and sharing ideas. It's an ideal time to toast to new beginnings and make resolutions, as your mind is agile and adaptable under this lunar influence.

**1 Thursday**

On New Year's Day, Mercury ingresses into Capricorn while squaring Neptune, and you may encounter a blend of practicality and dreaminess in your thinking and communication. This combination could lead to some challenges as you strive to set realistic goals and plans for the year ahead while also navigating moments of confusion or miscommunication. Maintaining a clear and organized mindset is helpful, as Capricorn's influence encourages structure and discipline.

# Astrology, Tarot & Horoscope Books.

Mystic Cat

Ohoroscope@Hotmail.com

www.ingramcontent.com/pod-product-compliance
Lightning Source LLC
Chambersburg PA
CBHW080530090426
42733CB00015B/2542
*9781922813442*